low-fat microwave meals

microwave cooking library®

by barbara methven

Dietary Guidelines

Carbohydrates
At least 50% of
total calories

The American Heart Association's
current *Dietary Guidelines for
Healthy American Adults* suggests
a preventive diet for coronary
heart disease. These guidelines
propose a reduction, not only of
dietary cholesterol and saturated
fat, but of all fats in the diet. They
recommend replacing fat calories with complex carbohydrates.
The guidelines are printed here
with the permission of the American Heart Association.

1. Total fat intake should be less
than 30% of calories.

2. Saturated fat intake should be
less than 10% of calories.

3. Polyunsaturated
fat intake should not
exceed 10% of calories.

4. Cholesterol intake should not
exceed 300 mg. per day.

5. Carbohydrate intake should
constitute 50% or more of calories, with emphasis on complex
carbohydrates.

6. Protein intake should provide
the remainder of the calories.

7. Sodium intake should not exceed 3000 mg. per day.

8. Alcoholic consumption should
not exceed 1 to 2 ounces of
ethanol per day. Two ounces of
100-proof whiskey, 8 ounces of
wine or 24 ounces of beer each
contain 1 ounce of ethanol.

Fats
Less than 30% of total calories

Protein
15% of total calories

9. Total calories should be sufficient to maintain the individual's recommended body weight.*

10. A wide variety of foods should be consumed.

* *Metropolitan Tables of Height and Weight, Table of Desirable Weights for Men and Women*. Metropolitan Life Insurance Company, New York, 1959.

One teaspoon salt has 2132 mg. sodium.

One large egg has 274 mg. cholesterol.

Appetizers & Snacks

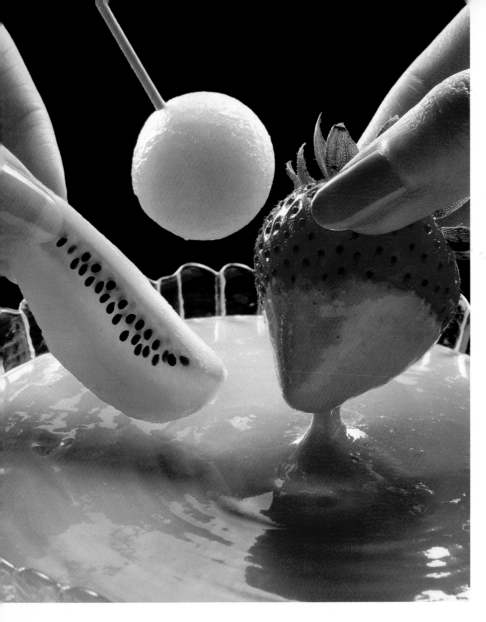

Hot Pepper Cheese Spread

1 tablespoon water
2 teaspoons dehydrated sweet
  bell pepper flakes
8 oz. hard farmer cheese, cut
  into 1-inch cubes
4 oz. light cream cheese
  (Neufchâtel), cut into 1-inch
  cubes
½ teaspoon crushed red
  pepper flakes

12 servings, 1 oz. each

In small bowl, place water and bell pepper flakes. Cover with plastic wrap. Microwave at High for 30 to 45 seconds, or until warm. Let stand, covered, until peppers are rehydrated.

In medium mixing bowl, micro-wave cheeses at 30% (Medium Low) for 3 to 4 minutes, or until slightly softened, stirring cheeses and rotating bowl every 30 seconds. (Watch carefully to avoid melting.) Mash cheeses with pastry blender or fork until smooth. Stir in rehydrated peppers and red pepper flakes. Pack mixture into cheese crock or small mixing bowl. Cover with plastic wrap. Chill at least 4 hours, or until firm. Serve as spread with melba toast rounds.

Per Serving:	
Calories:	93
Protein:	5 g.
Carbohydrate:	1 g.
Fat (total):	8 g.
Saturated Fat:	5 g.
Cholesterol:	25 mg.
Sodium:	123 mg.
Fiber:	—
Exchanges:	1 lean meat, 1 fat

Raspberry Fruit Dip ▲

1 cup frozen unsweetened
  raspberries
4 oz. light cream cheese
  (Neufchâtel)

½ cup vanilla-flavored low-fat
  yogurt

8 servings, 2 tbsp. each

In 1-quart casserole, microwave raspberries at High for 1 to 1½ minutes, or until defrosted, stirring once. Set aside.

In small mixing bowl, microwave cheese at High for 30 to 45 seconds, or until softened. In food processor or blender, combine raspberries, cream cheese and yogurt. Process until smooth. Serve with fresh pineapple chunks, strawberries, melon balls, kiwifruit wedges and grapes as dippers.

Per Serving:			
Calories:	82	Cholesterol:	11 mg.
Protein:	2 g.	Sodium:	67 mg.
Carbohydrate:	11 g.	Fiber:	2 g.
Fat (total):	4 g.	Exchanges:	½ fruit, ½ low-fat milk
Saturated Fat:	2 g.		

Tangy Vegetable Dip

¼ cup finely chopped carrot
¼ cup finely chopped green pepper
2 tablespoons finely chopped onion
2 tablespoons water
1 cup low-fat cottage cheese
¼ cup plain low-fat or nonfat yogurt
2 tablespoons fresh lemon juice

2 teaspoons dried dill weed
¼ teaspoon garlic powder
¼ teaspoon paprika
⅛ teaspoon cayenne
1 large carrot, cut into 4 × ½-inch spears
1 medium cucumber, cut into 4 × ½-inch spears
1 medium jicama, cut into 4 × ½-inch spears

Per Serving:	
Calories:	36
Protein:	3 g.
Carbohydrate:	5 g.
Fat (total):	1 g.
Saturated Fat:	—
Cholesterol:	2 mg.
Sodium:	84 mg.
Fiber:	1 g.
Exchanges:	1 vegetable

12 servings, 2 tbsp. each

How to Microwave Tangy Vegetable Dip

Combine carrot, green pepper, onion and water in 1-quart casserole. Cover. Microwave at High for 2 to 3 minutes, or until vegetables are tender-crisp, stirring once. Drain. Set aside.

Place cottage cheese, yogurt and lemon juice in food processor or blender. Process until smooth. Place in small mixing bowl. Add cooked vegetables and dill weed. Mix well. Cover with plastic wrap and chill.

Combine garlic powder, paprika and cayenne in small bowl. Arrange carrot, cucumber and jicama spears on serving platter. Sprinkle with spice mixture. Serve vegetables with dip.

◄ Layered Lentil Loaf

Nonstick vegetable cooking
   spray
3 cups hot water
1 cup dried lentils, rinsed and
    drained
½ cup chopped onion
3 teaspoons low-sodium beef
    bouillon granules
2 large cloves garlic
2 tablespoons water, divided
1 cup frozen sliced carrots
1 teaspoon dried thyme leaves
1 cup frozen peas
1 teaspoon dried sage leaves

Two loaves (2 cups each)

Spray two 5¾ × 3¼-inch alu-
minum foil pans with nonstick
vegetable cooking spray. Set
aside. Continue with photo directions, opposite.

Per Serving:	
Calories:	57
Protein:	4 g.
Carbohydrate:	10 g.
Fat (total):	—
Saturated Fat:	—
Cholesterol:	—
Sodium:	19 mg.
Fiber:	1 g.
Exchanges:	½ starch, ½ vegetable

Mosaic French Bread Pizza

1 loaf (1 lb.) French bread, cut
    in half crosswise

Sauce:
1 can (7½ oz.) whole tomatoes,
    cut up and undrained
1 teaspoon olive oil
½ teaspoon dried basil leaves
⅛ teaspoon garlic powder

1 yellow summer squash
    (about 6 oz.), cut into
    ¼-inch slices (1½ cups)
1 zucchini (about 6 oz.), cut
    into ¼-inch slices (1½ cups)
2 tablespoons water
2 Roma tomatoes, sliced,
    ¼-inch slices
½ cup shredded hard farmer
    cheese (2 oz.)

8 servings

Wrap half of French bread loaf in foil. Freeze for future use. Slice remaining half lengthwise. Set aside. In 1-quart casserole, combine all sauce
ingredients. Microwave at High, uncovered, for 8 to 10 minutes, or until
sauce is thickened, stirring 2 or 3 times. Set aside.

In another 1-quart casserole or small mixing bowl, place squash, zucchini and water. Cover. Microwave at High for 3 to 4 minutes, or until
tender-crisp, stirring once. Drain. Set aside.

Place French bread halves cut-sides-up under conventional broiler, 4
to 5 inches from heat. Broil until golden brown, 2 to 3 minutes. Spread
each toasted loaf half with half of tomato sauce. Arrange half of squash
mixture and tomato slices, slightly overlapping, on each loaf half.
Sprinkle evenly with cheese.

Place 1 French bread pizza on paper-towel-lined plate. Microwave at
High for 1 to 2 minutes, or until cheese is melted, rotating once. Repeat with remaining pizza. Cut each pizza crosswise into quarters.

Per Serving:				
Calories:	107		Cholesterol:	1 mg.
Protein:	4 g.		Sodium:	239 mg.
Carbohydrate:	19 g.		Fiber:	2 g.
Fat (total):	2 g.		Exchanges:	1 starch, 1 vegetable
Saturated Fat:	—			

How to Microwave Layered Lentil Loaf (Recipe not recommended for ovens with less than 600 watts.)

Combine 3 cups water, the lentils, onion, bouillon and garlic in 3-quart casserole. Cover. Microwave at High for 10 minutes. Microwave at 50% (Medium) for 30 minutes longer.

Remove cover. Stir. Microwave at 50% (Medium) for 25 to 30 minutes, or until lentils are tender and mixture is stiff but not dry. Let stand, covered, for 10 minutes.

Process cooked lentils until smooth in food processor or blender. Place in medium mixing bowl. Cover with plastic wrap. Set aside.

Place 1 tablespoon water, the carrots and thyme in 1-quart casserole. Cover. Microwave at High for 9 to 10 minutes, or until very tender. Mash with pastry blender or fork. Re-cover. Set aside.

Place remaining 1 tablespoon water, the peas and sage in small mixing bowl. Cover with plastic wrap. Microwave at High for 5 to 6 minutes, or until very tender. Mash with pastry blender or fork.

Spoon heaping ⅓ cup lentil mixture into each prepared loaf pan. Spread in even layer. Top each lentil layer evenly with carrot mixture. Spread in even layer.

Spoon another heaping ⅓ cup lentils into each pan. Spread in even layer. Top each lentil layer evenly with pea mixture. Spread in even layer.

Divide remaining lentil mixture in half and spread evenly over pea mixture in each pan. Cover each loaf with plastic wrap and refrigerate at least 8 hours.

Loosen around edges with knife. Invert onto serving plate. Serve with crackers. Wrap and freeze remaining loaf up to 1 month, if desired. Defrost in refrigerator before inverting onto serving plate.

Tropical Fruit & Cheese Log

◄

- 1 can (8 oz.) crushed pineapple, in juice
- 4 oz. light cream cheese (Neufchâtel)
- ½ cup chopped dried apricots
- 2 tablespoons finely chopped cashews
- 2 tablespoons poppy seeds

16 servings

Drain pineapple, pressing to remove excess moisture. Discard juice. In medium mixing bowl, microwave cheese at High for 30 to 45 seconds, or until softened. Add pineapple, apricots and cashews. Mix well.

On sheet of wax paper, form cheese mixture into 8-inch log. Sprinkle evenly with poppy seeds, rolling log to coat all sides. Wrap cheese log with wax paper. Refrigerate at least 8 hours, or until firm. To serve, cut into sixteen ½-inch slices. Serve with crackers or apple wedges, if desired.

NOTE: Tropical Fruit & Cheese Log may be served as a spread for bagels.

Per Serving:	
Calories:	45
Protein:	1 g.
Carbohydrate:	5 g.
Fat (total):	3 g.
Saturated Fat:	1 g.
Cholesterol:	5 mg.
Sodium:	29 mg.
Fiber:	1 g.
Exchanges:	½ fruit, ½ fat

Artichokes with Hungarian Dipping Sauce

- 2 fresh artichokes (8 to 10 oz. each)
- 2 tablespoons lemon juice
- 1 cup low-fat cottage cheese
- 2 tablespoons low-fat buttermilk
- 1 teaspoon grated lemon peel
- ½ teaspoon paprika
- 1 lemon, quartered

8 servings

Trim stems close to base of each artichoke. Cut 1 inch off tops, and trim ends off each leaf. Cut each artichoke lengthwise into quarters. Remove some of center leaves, and scrape out choke from each piece. Brush with lemon juice to prevent darkening.

Arrange artichoke quarters around edge of 10 to 12-inch platter, with heart of artichoke toward outside. Cover with plastic wrap. Microwave at High for 8 to 12 minutes, or until tender, rotating platter twice. Let stand, covered, for 5 minutes.

In food processor or blender, place remaining ingredients except lemon. Process until smooth. Place mixture in small bowl. Serve artichokes warm or cold with sauce and lemon wedges.

Per Serving:			
Calories:	43	Cholesterol:	2 mg.
Protein:	5 g.	Sodium:	141 mg.
Carbohydrate:	5 g.	Fiber:	2 g.
Fat (total):	1 g.	Exchanges:	1½ vegetable
Saturated Fat:	—		

Corn, Cucumber & Avocado Salsa ▶

1   can (7 oz.) corn, rinsed and
     drained
¼ cup sliced green onions
1   teaspoon olive oil
½ teaspoon cumin seed,
     crushed
½ teaspoon dried oregano
     leaves
1   cup seeded chopped
     cucumber
1   cup seeded chopped tomato
1   tablespoon white wine
     vinegar
1   tablespoon lime juice
¼ cup diced avocado

12 servings, ¼ cup each

In 1-quart casserole, combine
corn, onions, olive oil, cumin seed
and oregano. Cover. Microwave
at High for 1½ to 2 minutes, or until onions are tender, stirring once.
Add cucumber, tomato and vinegar. Mix well. Re-cover and chill
at least 2 hours to blend flavors.

In small mixing bowl, place lime
juice. Add diced avocado. Toss
to coat. Remove from bowl with
slotted spoon. Discard lime juice.
Sprinkle avocado over top of salsa
mixture. Serve with Seasoned
Whole Wheat Tortilla Chips (right),
if desired.

Per Serving:	
Calories:	22
Protein:	1 g.
Carbohydrate:	3 g.
Fat (total):	1 g.
Saturated Fat:	—
Cholesterol:	—
Sodium:	34 mg.
Fiber:	1 g.
Exchanges:	1 vegetable

Seasoned Whole Wheat Tortilla Chips ▲

Nonstick vegetable cooking
   spray
3 whole wheat flour tortillas
     (8-inch)

½ teaspoon ground cumin
¼ teaspoon ground oregano
¼ teaspoon paprika

6 servings, 4 chips each

Heat conventional oven to 375°F. Spray large baking sheet with nonstick
vegetable cooking spray. Set aside.

Cut each flour tortilla into 8 wedges. In large plastic food-storage bag,
place seasonings. Add tortilla wedges. Shake bag to coat chips with
seasonings.

Arrange chips in single layer on prepared baking sheet. Bake for 13
to 15 minutes, or until light golden brown. Place chips on cooling rack.
Cool completely.

Per Serving:			
Calories:	33	Cholesterol:	—
Protein:	1 g.	Sodium:	—
Carbohydrate:	7 g.	Fiber:	—
Fat (total):	—	Exchanges:	½ starch
Saturated Fat:			

Cheese & Vegetable Nachos

1 recipe Seasoned Whole
   Wheat Tortilla Chips
   (page 25)

Bean Mixture:

1 can (16 oz.) pinto beans,
   rinsed and drained
¼ cup finely chopped onion
1 tablespoon water
1 large clove garlic, minced
1 teaspoon olive oil
½ teaspoon paprika
¼ teaspoon ground cumin
⅛ teaspoon ground oregano

24 fresh broccoli flowerets
   (about 8 oz.)
½ cup chopped red pepper
1 tablespoon water
½ cup shredded hard farmer
   cheese (2 oz.), divided

6 servings, 4 nachos each

Prepare chips as directed. Cool completely. Set aside.

Place bean mixture ingredients in 1-quart casserole. Cover. Microwave at High for 2 to 4 minutes, or until onion is tender, stirring once. Mash bean mixture with fork. Set aside.

In 1-quart casserole or small mixing bowl, combine broccoli, red pepper and water. Cover. Microwave at High for 1½ to 3 minutes, or until vegetables are hot and colors brighten, stirring once. Rinse with cold water. Drain.

Spread each of 12 chips with 2 teaspoons bean mixture. Arrange chips in even layer on plate. Top each chip with 1 broccoli floweret. Sprinkle chips evenly with half of red pepper and half of cheese. Microwave at High for 1½ to 2½ minutes, or until cheese is melted. Serve immediately. Repeat with remaining chips.

Per Serving:			
Calories:	149	Cholesterol:	9 mg.
Protein:	8 g.	Sodium:	55 mg.
Carbohydrate:	21 g.	Fiber:	6 g.
Fat (total):	4 g.	Exchanges:	1 starch, ½ lean meat,
Saturated Fat:	2 g.		1 vegetable, ½ fat

Thai-style Skewered Chicken

½ cup white wine vinegar
¼ cup sugar
⅛ teaspoon salt
½ cup peeled and coarsely chopped cucumber
½ cup water
3 tablespoons low-sodium soy sauce
2 tablespoons lemon juice
2 teaspoons peanut butter

1 teaspoon grated fresh gingerroot
¼ teaspoon cayenne
¼ teaspoon curry powder
1 boneless whole chicken breast (8 to 10 oz.), cut into 24 pieces
6 green onions, trimmed and each cut into 3 lengths (1½-inch)
6 wooden skewers, 6-inch

6 servings

Per Serving:				
Calories:	103	Cholesterol:	30 mg.	
Protein:	12 g.	Sodium:	154 mg.	
Carbohydrate:	11 g.	Fiber:	1 g.	
Fat (total):	2 g.	Exchanges:	1 lean meat, 1 vegetable, ½ fruit	
Saturated Fat:	—			

How to Microwave Thai-style Skewered Chicken

Combine vinegar, sugar and salt in 2-cup measure. Microwave at High for 1½ to 2 minutes, or until mixture boils and sugar dissolves. Cool slightly.

Place cucumber in medium mixing bowl. Pour vinegar mixture over cucumber. Cover with plastic wrap. Chill until serving time.

Combine water, soy sauce, juice, peanut butter, gingerroot, cayenne and curry powder in 2-cup measure. Stir with whisk until peanut butter dissolves. Set aside.

Thread 4 chicken pieces and 3 green onion pieces alternately on each of 6 wooden skewers. Place kabobs in 8-inch square baking dish.

Pour soy sauce mixture over kabobs. Cover with plastic wrap. Marinate in refrigerator at least 8 hours or overnight, turning kabobs once or twice.

Microwave kabobs, covered, in marinade at High for 3 to 6 minutes, or until chicken is no longer pink, turning over once. Remove from marinade. Discard marinade. Serve kabobs with sauce.

Cheese & Basil Pepper Spirals

1 red pepper (about 8 oz.)
2 oz. light cream cheese (Neufchâtel)
½ teaspoon dried basil leaves
⅛ teaspoon garlic powder
Dash to ⅛ teaspoon cayenne

6 servings, 4 spirals each

Per Serving:	
Calories:	35
Protein:	1 g.
Carbohydrate:	2 g.
Fat (total):	2 g.
Saturated Fat:	1 g.
Cholesterol:	7 mg.
Sodium:	39 mg.
Fiber:	1 g.
Exchanges:	½ vegetable, ½ fat

How to Make Cheese & Basil Pepper Spirals

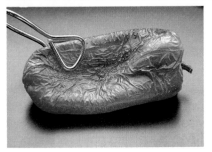

Place red pepper on baking sheet. Place under conventional broiler 4 to 5 inches from heat. Broil for 15 to 18 minutes, or until skin of pepper blisters and darkens, turning several times. (Skin may blacken in some areas.)

Place pepper in brown paper bag, using tongs. Roll top down tightly. Let pepper sweat for 15 minutes in bag. Remove pepper from bag. Using thin-bladed knife, peel off skin, working in sections from top to bottom.

Cut peeled pepper in half lengthwise. Remove core and seeds. Make tiny slits in bottom of each pepper half so halves lie flat. Place on paper towels. Gently pat dry. Set aside.

Place cheese in small bowl. Microwave at High for 15 to 30 seconds, or until softened. Stir in basil, garlic powder and cayenne. Divide cream cheese mixture in half.

Place each pepper half on sheet of plastic wrap. Spread each pepper half evenly with cheese mixture. Starting with longer side, roll up peppers, jelly roll style, using plastic wrap to lift and roll.

Wrap each roll-up in plastic wrap. Chill 2 hours, or until firm. Slice each roll-up into 12 spirals. Serve spirals on melba toast rounds or cucumber slices.

Feta & Pepper Crisps ▶

1 tablespoon snipped fresh
   parsley
2 teaspoons olive oil
1 teaspoon dried basil leaves
1 clove garlic, minced
½ teaspoon dried rosemary
   leaves, crushed
½ cup green pepper strips
   (1 × ¼-inch strips)
½ cup red pepper strips
   (1 × ¼-inch strips)
2 tablespoons chopped onion
2 whole wheat pitas (4-inch)
1 tablespoon feta cheese,
   crumbled

4 servings

In small bowl, combine parsley,
oil, basil, garlic and rosemary.
Mix well. Set aside.

In 1-quart casserole, place peppers and onion. Cover. Microwave
at High for 4 to 5 minutes, or until
peppers are tender. Set aside.

Cut each pita in half crosswise
to make 2 separate circles. Toast
pita halves. Place toasted halves
on 10-inch round platter. Brush
each evenly with parsley mixture.
Spoon pepper mixture evenly
onto pita halves. Sprinkle with
feta cheese. Microwave at High
for 30 seconds to 1 minute, or
until cheese is melted and crisps
are warm.

Per Serving:	
Calories:	78
Protein:	2 g.
Carbohydrate:	11 g.
Fat (total):	3 g.
Saturated Fat:	1 g.
Cholesterol:	2 mg.
Sodium:	22 mg.
Fiber:	1 g.
Exchanges:	½ starch,
	½ vegetable, ½ fat

Garlic-Chive Potato Crisps

Nonstick vegetable cooking
   spray
1 russet potato (6 oz.)

2 teaspoons snipped fresh
   chives
⅛ teaspoon garlic powder
⅛ teaspoon salt

4 servings, about 6 crisps each

Heat conventional oven to 425°F. Spray 15½ × 10½-inch jelly roll pan
with nonstick vegetable cooking spray. Set aside.

Using thin slicing blade of food processor or very sharp knife, cut
potato into ⅛-inch slices. Place slices in bowl of ice water to prevent
darkening. Let stand for 15 minutes.

Remove potato slices from water and blot dry with paper towels. Arrange slices in single layer on prepared pan.

In small bowl, combine chives, garlic powder and salt. Sprinkle evenly
over potato slices. Bake for 15 to 20 minutes, or until crisps are brown,
rearranging twice during baking and removing as they brown. Place
browned crisps on cooling rack. Cool completely.

Per Serving:			
Calories:	35	Cholesterol:	—
Protein:	1 g.	Sodium:	68 mg.
Carbohydrate:	8 g.	Fiber:	1 g.
Fat (total):	—	Exchanges:	½ starch
Saturated Fat:	—		

Soups & Broths

Making your own soup stock guarantees that the broth will be low-fat, low-sodium and flavor-rich. Freeze extra broth in 1-cup amounts for up to 6 months. Use an ice cube tray to freeze broth cubes (about 2 tablespoons each). Use one or two cubes, defrosted, for stir-fries or other recipes that call for small amounts of broth.

Low-fat Vegetable Broth

1 bouquet garni (below)
1 tablespoon margarine
1 leek, cut in half lengthwise, rinsed, sliced
4 carrots, cut into 1-inch chunks
1 cup coarsely chopped celery*
8 oz. fresh mushrooms
1 turnip (8 oz.), peeled and cubed (1-inch cubes)
3 small onions, unpeeled, cut in half lengthwise
10 cups water
½ teaspoon salt
2 whole cloves

8 cups

Prepare bouquet garni as directed. Set aside. In 4-quart Dutch oven, melt margarine conventionally over medium heat. Add leek, carrots, celery, mushrooms, turnip and onions. Sauté over medium heat for 5 to 8 minutes, or until vegetables are tender-crisp.

Add bouquet garni, water, salt and cloves. Reduce heat to low. Cover partially. Simmer, do not boil, over low heat for 1½ to 2 hours. Strain stock. Discard vegetables. Place strained broth in 8-cup measure. Cover and chill 4 hours. Remove solid fat from top.

Freeze broth in 1-cup amounts or in ice cube trays. Label and date packages. Freeze up to 6 months, if desired. To defrost broth, microwave as directed in chart, page 37.

*For better-flavored broth, use inner, leafy portion of celery stalk.

Because all solids are strained from broth, nutritional information cannot be calculated.

How to Make Bouquet Garni

Assemble 4 sprigs fresh parsley, 3 to 4 sprigs fresh thyme, 1 large bay leaf and 1 large clove garlic, cut in half lengthwise.

Cut two 4-inch pieces from outer layer of halved and washed leek. Place herbs and garlic on concave side of 1 piece.

Cover with remaining piece of leek. Tie in 3 places with string to secure seasoning bundle.

Chicken & Shrimp Gumbo

¼ cup all-purpose flour
2¼ cups Low-fat Chicken Broth (page 36) or defatted chicken broth, divided
¾ cup chopped celery
¾ cup chopped green pepper
¾ cup chopped onion
2 large cloves garlic, minced
1 can (28 oz.) whole. tomatoes, undrained and cut up
1 cup shredded cooked chicken
3 tablespoons snipped fresh parsley
½ teaspoon dried thyme leaves
¼ to ½ teaspoon pepper
Dash red pepper sauce
½ lb. medium shrimp, shelled and deveined (about 20)

6 servings, 1 cup each

Heat conventional oven to 400°F. Sprinkle flour evenly into 8-inch square baking pan. Bake for 10 to 15 minutes, or until flour is deep golden brown, stirring every 5 minutes. Set aside.

In 3-quart casserole, place ¼ cup broth, the celery, green pepper, onion and garlic. Cover. Microwave at High for 3 to 5 minutes, or until vegetables are tender-crisp, stirring once. Stir in browned flour. Blend in remaining 2 cups broth, the tomatoes, chicken, parsley, thyme, pepper, and red pepper sauce. Microwave at High, uncovered, for 12 to 15 minutes, or until mixture begins to boil, stirring 3 times. Add shrimp. Microwave at 50% (Medium) for 3 to 5 minutes, or until shrimp are firm and opaque.

Per Serving:	
Calories:	147
Protein:	17 g.
Carbohydrate:	14 g.
Fat (total):	3 g.
Saturated Fat:	1 g.
Cholesterol:	78 mg.
Sodium:	307 mg.
Fiber:	2 g.
Exchanges:	1½ lean meat, 3 vegetable

Creamy Potato & Wild Rice Soup ▶

5 cups water, divided
½ cup uncooked wild rice
4 potatoes (6 oz. each), peeled and cubed (½-inch cubes), about 4 cups
1 cup chopped onion
½ cup shredded carrot
½ teaspoon salt
¼ teaspoon pepper
2 tablespoons snipped fresh parsley

6 servings, 1 cup each

In 2-quart saucepan, combine 2 cups water and the rice. Bring to boil conventionally over high heat. Reduce heat to low. Cover. Simmer for 30 to 35 minutes, or until rice kernels are open and almost all liquid is absorbed. Let stand, covered, for 15 minutes. Drain. Set aside.

In 3-quart casserole, place potatoes, onion and ½ cup water. Cover. Microwave at High for 15 to 20 minutes, or until potatoes are very tender, stirring twice. Place 3 cups of potato mixture in food processor or blender. Process until smooth. Add back to potatoes in casserole. Add remaining 2½ cups water, the cooked rice, the carrot, salt and pepper. Mix well. Re-cover. Microwave at High for 5 to 10 minutes, or until soup is hot and carrot is tender, stirring once. Garnish each serving evenly with parsley.

Per Serving:	
Calories:	149
Protein:	4 g.
Carbohydrate:	34 g.
Fat (total):	—
Saturated Fat:	—
Cholesterol:	—
Sodium:	191 mg.
Fiber:	3 g.
Exchanges:	1½ starch, 2 vegetable

Curry Chicken & Apple Soup

1 Granny Smith apple, cored and chopped
2 medium carrots, thinly sliced
½ cup thinly sliced celery
½ cup chopped green pepper
⅓ cup chopped onion
1 teaspoon margarine
1 teaspoon curry powder
½ teaspoon salt
¼ teaspoon grated lemon peel
¼ teaspoon ground cloves

3 cups Low-fat Chicken or Vegetable Broth (pages 35 and 36) or defatted chicken broth
1 can (16 oz.) whole tomatoes, undrained and cut up
1 boneless whole chicken breast (8 to 10 oz.), skin removed, cut into thin strips (1½-inch strips)

8 servings, 1 cup each

In 3-quart casserole, combine apple, carrots, celery, pepper, onion, margarine, curry powder, salt, peel and cloves. Mix well. Cover. Microwave at High for 4 to 6 minutes, or until vegetables are tender, stirring once or twice. Add remaining ingredients. Mix well. Re-cover. Microwave at High for 14 to 18 minutes, or until chicken is no longer pink and soup is hot, stirring 2 or 3 times.

Per Serving:			
Calories:	80	Cholesterol:	21 mg.
Protein:	9 g.	Sodium:	265 mg.
Carbohydrate:	8 g.	Fiber:	2 g.
Fat (total):	2 g.	Exchanges:	1 lean meat, 1½ vegetable
Saturated Fat:	—		

◄ Crab Bisque

    8 oz. fresh mushrooms, sliced
    ¼ cup white wine
    ¼ cup all-purpose flour
    ½ teaspoon salt
    ¼ teaspoon white pepper
    3 cups skim milk
    1 can (12 oz.) evaporated skim
       milk
    1 can (8 oz.) whole tomatoes,
       drained and chopped
    1 can (6 oz.) crab meat, rinsed,
       drained and cartilage
       removed
    1 tablespoon snipped fresh
       parsley

        6 servings, 1 cup each

In 3-quart casserole, place mushrooms and white wine. Cover. Microwave at High for 5 to 6 minutes, or until mushrooms are tender, stirring once. Stir in flour, salt and pepper. Blend in milks. Microwave, uncovered, at High for 9 to 12 minutes, or until mixture thickens slightly and bubbles, stirring 2 or 3 times with whisk. Add remaining ingredients. Cover. Microwave at High for 3 to 5 minutes, or until soup is hot, stirring once.

Per Serving:	
Calories:	157
Protein:	15 g.
Carbohydrate:	21 g.
Fat (total):	1 g.
Saturated Fat:	—
Cholesterol:	25 mg.
Sodium:	454 mg.
Fiber:	1 g.
Exchanges:	1 lean meat,
	1 vegetable,
	1 skim milk

Cold Lemon Cucumber Soup

    3 medium cucumbers,
       peeled, seeded and sliced
       (about 4 cups)
 2½ cups low-fat buttermilk
    1 cup plain low-fat or nonfat
       yogurt
    ¼ cup sliced green onions
    1 teaspoon grated lemon peel

        6 servings, ¾ cup each

In large mixing bowl, combine all ingredients. Place half of mixture in food processor or blender. Process until smooth. Repeat with remaining mixture. Chill at least 4 hours. Garnish with lemon slices, if desired.

Per Serving:			
Calories:	83	Cholesterol:	6 mg.
Protein:	6 g.	Sodium:	138 mg.
Carbohydrate:	11 g.	Fiber:	1 g.
Fat (total):	2 g.	Exchanges:	1 vegetable, ½ skim milk
Saturated Fat:	1 g.		

Saffron Squash & Leek Soup ▲

½ cup sliced leek, washed
1 teaspoon margarine
¼ teaspoon salt
⅛ teaspoon garlic powder
⅛ teaspoon white pepper
   (optional)
1 pkg. (12 oz.) frozen cooked
   winter squash
1 can (12 oz.) evaporated skim
   milk
1 cup low-fat buttermilk
¼ teaspoon saffron threads

   4 servings, 1 cup each

In 2-quart casserole, place leek, margarine, salt, garlic powder and pepper. Cover. Microwave at High for 1 to 3 minutes, or until margarine is melted and leek is tender. Add squash. Re-cover. Microwave at High for 2 to 4 minutes, or until squash is defrosted, stirring once or twice to break apart. Add remaining ingredients. Mix well. Re-cover. Microwave at High for 7 to 9 minutes, or until soup is hot, stirring twice.

Per Serving:			
Calories:	149	Cholesterol:	5 mg.
Protein:	10 g.	Sodium:	318 mg.
Carbohydrate:	25 g.	Fiber:	2 g.
Fat (total):	2 g.	Exchanges:	1 starch, ½ low-fat milk
Saturated Fat:	1 g.		

Yellow Split Pea & Vegetable Soup

6 cups Low-fat Vegetable Broth
   (page 35)
1 cup dried yellow split peas
½ cup chopped onion
1 clove garlic
½ teaspoon salt
¼ teaspoon dried marjoram
   leaves
⅛ teaspoon cayenne
1 cup sliced carrots
1 cup sliced parsnips
½ cup sliced celery

   8 servings, 1 cup each

In 3-quart casserole, combine broth, peas, onion, garlic, salt, marjoram and cayenne. Cover. Microwave at High for 10 minutes. Microwave at 50% (Medium) for 20 minutes longer. Add carrots, parsnips and celery. Re-cover. Microwave at 50% (Medium) for 25 to 35 minutes, or until peas are very tender, stirring once.

Per Serving:			
Calories:	111	Cholesterol:	—
Protein:	7 g.	Sodium:	159 mg.
Carbohydrate:	21 g.	Fiber:	2 g.
Fat (total):	—	Exchanges:	1 starch, 1 vegetable
Saturated Fat:	—		

Manhattan Clam Stew

- 2 cups vegetable juice cocktail
- 1 can (16 oz.) tomatoes, cut up and undrained
- 1 cup hot water
- 1 medium potato (6 oz.), cut into ½-inch cubes (about 1 cup)
- ¾ cup thinly sliced carrot
- ½ cup thinly sliced celery
- ½ cup broken uncooked spaghetti
- 2 cloves garlic, minced
- 1 teaspoon low-sodium beef bouillon granules
- ½ teaspoon Italian seasoning
- 1 lb. small steamer clams, scrubbed

6 servings, 1 cup each

In 3-quart casserole, combine all ingredients, except clams. Cover. Microwave at High for 10 minutes. Stir. Add clams. Re-cover. Microwave at High for 20 to 25 minutes, or until clams are open and vegetables and spaghetti are tender, stirring twice. Discard any unopened clams.

Per Serving:	
Calories:	99
Protein:	5 g.
Carbohydrate:	20 g.
Fat (total):	1 g.
Saturated Fat:	—
Cholesterol:	5 mg.
Sodium:	442 mg.
Fiber:	2 g.
Exchanges:	1 starch, 1 vegetable

Turkey Sausage & Bean Soup

½ lb. ground turkey (85% lean)
2 tablespoons snipped fresh parsley
½ teaspoon fennel seed, crushed
½ teaspoon dried oregano leaves
¼ teaspoon paprika
1½ cups thinly sliced carrots
1 cup thinly sliced zucchini
½ cup chopped onion
2 tablespoons water
4 cups Low-fat Chicken or Vegetable Broth (pages 35 and 36), or defatted chicken broth
1 can (15 oz.) white kidney beans, rinsed and drained
1 can (15 oz.) red kidney beans, rinsed and drained
½ teaspoon salt

8 servings, 1 cup each

In medium mixing bowl, combine turkey, parsley, fennel, oregano and paprika. Drop turkey sausage mixture by heaping teaspoons into 2-quart casserole. Microwave at High for 4 to 5 minutes, or until no longer pink, stirring once. Drain. Set aside.

In 3-quart casserole, combine carrots, zucchini, onion and water. Cover. Microwave at High for 9 to 12 minutes, or until carrots are tender, stirring once or twice. Add turkey sausage pieces, broth, beans and salt to vegetables. Re-cover. Microwave at High for 5 to 10 minutes, or until soup is hot, stirring once.

Per Serving:	
Calories:	141
Protein:	13 g.
Carbohydrate:	20 g.
Fat (total):	2 g.
Saturated Fat:	—
Cholesterol:	16 mg.
Sodium:	92 mg.
Fiber:	7 g.
Exchanges:	1 starch, 1 lean meat, 1 vegetable

Frosted Cranberry Soup ▲

1 pkg. (12 oz.) fresh cranberries
1 cup orange juice
⅓ cup sugar
¼ teaspoon ground cloves
⅛ teaspoon ground nutmeg
2½ cups low-fat buttermilk

6 servings, ¾ cup each

In 2-quart casserole, combine all ingredients except buttermilk. Cover. Microwave at High for 9 to 12 minutes, or until very hot and cranberries are split, stirring twice. Chill mixture until completely cool.

In food processor or blender, process cranberry mixture until smooth. Pour into large mixing bowl. Add buttermilk. Mix well. Cover with plastic wrap and chill 4 hours, or until serving time. Serve cold.

Per Serving:			
Calories:	131	Cholesterol:	4 mg.
Protein:	4 g.	Sodium:	108 mg.
Carbohydrate:	28 g.	Fiber:	3 g.
Fat (total):	1 g.	Exchanges:	1 fruit, 1 skim milk
Saturated Fat:	1 g.		

Lemon Broccoli & Cauliflower Salad

4 cups small fresh broccoli flowerets
2 cups small fresh cauliflowerets
½ cup water
¼ cup shredded carrot
2 tablespoons chopped red onion
2 tablespoons raisins
1 tablespoon sunflower nuts
½ cup plain low-fat or nonfat yogurt
1 tablespoon reduced-calorie mayonnaise
1 teaspoon honey
¼ teaspoon grated lemon peel

6 servings

In 2-quart casserole, combine broccoli, cauliflower and water. Cover. Microwave at High for 3 to 4 minutes, or until vegetables are very hot and color brightens. Rinse with cold water. Drain.

In large mixing bowl or salad bowl, combine broccoli and cauliflower, carrot, onion, raisins and sunflower nuts. Set aside.

In small mixing bowl, combine remaining ingredients. Mix well. Add yogurt mixture to vegetable mixture. Toss to coat. Cover salad with plastic wrap. Chill at least 4 hours or overnight to blend flavors.

Per Serving:	
Calories:	65
Protein:	4 g.
Carbohydrate:	11 g.
Fat (total):	2 g.
Saturated Fat:	—
Cholesterol:	1 mg.
Sodium:	51 mg.
Fiber:	3 g.
Exchanges:	2 vegetable, ½ fat

Cardamom Orange Spinach Salad ▶

Salad:
- 8 cups torn fresh spinach leaves
- 1 can (11 oz.) mandarin orange segments, drained
- ½ cup seedless red grapes, cut in half

Dressing:
- ½ cup plain low-fat or nonfat yogurt
- 2 teaspoons orange juice concentrate*
- 2 teaspoons honey
- ⅛ teaspoon ground cardamom

8 servings

In large mixing bowl or salad bowl, combine all salad ingredients. Set aside. In small mixing bowl, combine all dressing ingredients. Spoon 1 tablespoon dressing over each serving of salad.

*To defrost 1 can (6 oz.) frozen orange juice concentrate, remove top. Microwave at High for 45 seconds to 1 minute, or until partially defrosted. Let stand for 5 minutes to complete defrosting.

Per Serving:			
Calories:	45	Cholesterol:	—
Protein:	3 g.	Sodium:	56 mg.
Carbohydrate:	10 g.	Fiber:	2 g.
Fat (total):	—	Exchanges:	½ vegetable, ½ fruit
Saturated Fat:	—		

Honey-Raspberry Grapefruit Salad

- ½ cup frozen unsweetened raspberries
- 2 teaspoons honey
- 1½ teaspoons cornstarch
- ½ teaspoon grated lime peel
- 4 cups torn leaf lettuce
- 1 large pink grapefruit (18 oz.), peeled and sectioned (about 1 cup)

6 servings

Place raspberries in 1-quart casserole. Cover. Microwave at High for 45 seconds to 2 minutes, or until defrosted, checking once. Drain 1 tablespoon juice from raspberries, and place in 1-cup measure. Set raspberries aside.

Add water to juice to equal ½ cup. Add honey, cornstarch and lime peel. Stir to dissolve cornstarch. Microwave at High for 1½ to 2 minutes, or until mixture is thickened and translucent, stirring once or twice. Watch closely to prevent boilover.

Mash defrosted raspberries. Add thickened juice mixture. Mix well. Cover and chill 2 hours, or until serving time. In large mixing bowl or salad bowl, combine lettuce and grapefruit. Top each serving with 2 tablespoons dressing.

Per Serving:			
Calories:	50	Cholesterol:	—
Protein:	1 g.	Sodium:	5 mg.
Carbohydrate:	12 g.	Fiber:	2 g.
Fat (total):	—	Exchanges:	1 vegetable, ½ fruit
Saturated Fat:	—		

Oriental Scallop & Pasta Salad

4 oz. uncooked capellini (angel hair spaghetti), broken into 2-inch lengths

Dressing:
¼ cup white wine
2 tablespoons low-sodium soy sauce
2 tablespoons vegetable oil
1 teaspoon sugar
½ teaspoon grated orange peel
⅛ to ¼ teaspoon cayenne

1 lb. bay scallops
4 oz. fresh pea pods, thinly sliced (about 2 cups)
1 cup julienne carrot (2 × ⅛-inch strips)
1 small onion, cut in half lengthwise and thinly sliced (about ½ cup)
1 tablespoon water

6 servings

Prepare capellini as directed on package. Rinse with cold water. Drain. Cover and set aside.

In 1-cup measure, combine all dressing ingredients. Mix well. Set aside. In 8-inch round baking dish, arrange scallops in even layer. Cover with plastic wrap. Microwave at 70% (Medium High) for 5 to 8 minutes, or until scallops are opaque, stirring once. Let stand for 1 to 2 minutes. Drain. Set aside.

In 2-quart casserole, combine remaining ingredients. Cover. Microwave at High for 2 to 4 minutes, or until vegetables are tender-crisp, stirring once. Drain. Add cooked pasta, the dressing and scallops. Toss to combine. Re-cover and chill at least 4 hours. Toss again before serving.

Per Serving:			
Calories:	210	Cholesterol:	25 mg.
Protein:	16 g.	Sodium:	343 mg.
Carbohydrate:	22 g.	Fiber:	2 g.
Fat (total):	5 g.	Exchanges:	1 starch, 2 lean meat, 1 vegetable
Saturated Fat:	1 g.		

Crunchy Crab Salad in Tomato Cups

- 2 tablespoons slivered almonds
- 1 cup uncooked macaroni rings
- 2 tablespoons chopped celery
- 2 tablespoons chopped green pepper
- 2 tablespoons chopped onion
- 1 teaspoon grated lemon peel
- 1 can (6 oz.) crab meat, rinsed, drained and cartilage removed
- ½ cup plain low-fat or nonfat yogurt
- ⅛ teaspoon pepper
- 4 medium tomatoes

4 servings

Per Serving:	
Calories:	215
Protein:	14 g.
Carbohydrate:	34 g.
Fat (total):	3 g.
Saturated Fat:	—
Cholesterol:	26 mg.
Sodium:	133 mg.
Fiber:	3 g.
Exchanges:	1 starch,
	1 lean meat,
	3 vegetable

How to Make Crunchy Crab Salad in Tomato Cups

Heat conventional oven to 400°F. In 8-inch square baking pan, bake almonds for 5 to 7 minutes, or until toasted and light golden brown, stirring several times. Set aside. Prepare macaroni as directed on package. Rinse and drain. Set aside.

Combine celery, green pepper, onion and lemon peel in 1-quart casserole. Cover. Microwave at High for 1½ to 2 minutes, or until vegetables are tender-crisp, stirring once. In medium mixing bowl, combine toasted almonds, cooked macaroni, the vegetable mixture, crab meat, yogurt and pepper. Toss to coat. Cover with plastic wrap. Chill at least 2 hours.

Slice tomatoes into eighths, to within ¼ inch of base, being careful not to slice through. Spread sections out to form cup. Divide crab meat salad into fourths. Fill each tomato cup with one-fourth of salad.

Marinated Pork Medallion Salad

- 1 pork tenderloin (10 to 12 oz.), 5 inches in length
- ½ cup orange juice
- ½ teaspoon ground coriander
- ½ teaspoon pepper, divided
  Nonstick vegetable cooking spray
- ½ medium red onion, sliced
- ½ cup white wine vinegar
- 1 teaspoon grated orange peel
- 1 tablespoon plus 1 teaspoon olive oil
- 6 cups torn fresh spinach leaves
- 2 medium oranges, peeled and sectioned

4 servings

Per Serving:			
Calories:	217	Cholesterol:	62 mg.
Protein:	23 g.	Sodium:	112 mg.
Carbohydrate:	15 g.	Fiber:	4 g.
Fat (total):	8 g.	Exchanges:	2½ lean meat, 1½ vegetable, ½ fruit
Saturated Fat:	2 g.		

How to Make Marinated Pork Medallion Salad

Cut tenderloin crosswise into twenty ¼-inch slices. Place in large plastic food-storage bag. Add juice, coriander and ¼ teaspoon pepper. Secure bag. Marinate in refrigerator at least 1 hour.

Remove slices from marinade. Discard marinade. Flatten slices slightly with palm of hand. Spray 10-inch skillet with nonstick spray. Heat skillet conventionally over high heat. Brown slices for about 2 minutes on each side, or until no longer pink. Set aside.

Combine onion, vinegar, orange peel and remaining ¼ teaspoon pepper in 1-quart casserole. Cover. Microwave at High for 3 to 4 minutes, or until onion is soft and translucent. Blend in oil.

Arrange spinach, pork slices and orange sections evenly on each serving plate. Serve, topped evenly with warm dressing.

Grilled Chicken Salad

2 cups small fresh
  cauliflowerets
2 cups sliced yellow summer
  squash
2 tablespoons water
2 boneless whole chicken
  breasts (8 to 10 oz. each),
  split in half, skin removed
4 cups mixed salad greens
  (combination of Bibb, leaf
  and romaine lettuce)

Dressing:

½ cup low-fat buttermilk
1 tablespoon reduced-calorie
  mayonnaise
¼ teaspoon dried dill weed
¼ teaspoon dried parsley flakes
⅛ teaspoon garlic powder
⅛ teaspoon onion powder
⅛ teaspoon pepper

4 servings

In 2-quart casserole, place cauliflower, squash and water. Cover. Micro-wave at High for 5 to 8 minutes, or until vegetables are very hot and tender-crisp, stirring once. Drain. Set aside.

Grill chicken breasts conventionally over medium-high heat for 18 to 20 minutes, or until chicken is no longer pink and juices run clear, turning once. Arrange greens and vegetable mixture evenly on serving plates. Slice each breast half into 6 pieces and arrange 1 sliced breast half on each serving plate. In 2-cup measure, combine dressing ingredients. Blend with whisk. Top each serving with about 2 tablespoons dressing.

NOTE: If desired, arrange chicken breast halves in 8-inch square baking dish with thickest portions toward outside. Cover with wax paper. Microwave at High for 6 to 8 minutes, or until chicken is no longer pink and juices run clear, rearranging once or twice.

Per Serving:			
Calories:	218	Cholesterol:	86 mg.
Protein:	34 g.	Sodium:	139 mg.
Carbohydrate:	8 g.	Fiber:	3 g.
Fat (total):	5 g.	Exchanges:	3½ lean meat, 2 vegetable
Saturated Fat:	1 g.		

Main Dishes

Fish & Seafood

A variety of fresh fish is now available, even in inland markets. Most fish are exceptionally low in saturated fat and total fat, and relatively low in cholesterol. Even fatty fishes like herring and salmon compare well with skinned, dark meat poultry.

However, mackerel and pompano contain more saturated fat than any of the lean cuts of meat.

Shellfish, like veal, are very low in fat but higher in cholesterol. Shrimp and calamari (squid) contain very high amounts of cholesterol and should be eaten no more than once a week. (Portions evaluated were larger than those recommended by the American Heart Association.)

The following chart compares the saturated fat, cholesterol and total fat content of fish and seafood, ranking them from lower to higher saturated fat in each category.

Fats & Cholesterol Comparison of Fish & Seafood

Product (3½ ounces, cooked)	Saturated Fatty Acids (grams)	Cholesterol (milligrams)	Total Fat (grams)
Finfish			
Haddock	0.2	74	0.9
Cod, Atlantic	0.2	55	0.9
Pollock, walleye	0.2	96	1.1
Snapper, mixed species	0.4	47	1.7
Halibut, Atlantic and Pacific	0.4	41	2.9
Trout, rainbow	0.8	73	4.3
Swordfish	1.4	50	5.1
Tuna, bluefin	1.6	49	6.3
Salmon, sockeye	1.9	87	11.0
Mackerel, Atlantic	4.2	75	17.8
Pompano, Florida	4.5	64	12.1
Crustaceans			
Lobster, northern	0.1	72	0.6
Crab, blue	0.2	100	1.8
Shrimp, mixed species	0.3	195	1.1
Mollusks			
Scallops	0.08	33	0.4
Clam, mixed species	0.2	67	2.0
Squid	0.4	233	1.0

Source:

United States Department of Agriculture, Human Nutrition Information Service. Agriculture Handbook 8-15, *Composition of Foods: Finfish and Shellfish Products — Raw • Processed • Prepared.*

Tropical Sweet & Sour Swordfish

1 tablespoon plus 1 teaspoon
   flaked coconut
½ cup thinly sliced carrot
1 small onion, cut into 12
   wedges
¼ cup plus 2 tablespoons
   water, divided
2 tablespoons packed brown
   sugar
2 teaspoons cornstarch
¼ teaspoon low-sodium
   chicken bouillon granules
3 tablespoons white wine
   vinegar
2 tablespoons catsup
1 can (8 oz.) pineapple chunks
   in juice, drained
1 swordfish steak (12 oz.),
   about 1 inch thick, cut into
   4 serving-size pieces
1 tablespoon lemon juice
¼ teaspoon garlic powder

4 servings

Sprinkle coconut in 9-inch pie plate. Microwave at High for 2½ to 3½ minutes, or until lightly browned, tossing with fork after first minute and then every 30 seconds. Set aside.

In 1-quart casserole, place carrot, onion and 2 tablespoons water. Cover. Microwave at High for 2 to 4 minutes, or until vegetables are tender, stirring once. Drain.

Add sugar, cornstarch and bouillon. Mix well. Blend in remaining ¼ cup water, the vinegar and catsup. Stir in pineapple chunks. Microwave at High for 4 to 6 minutes, or until sauce is thickened and translucent, stirring every 2 minutes. Set aside.

In 8-inch square baking dish, place swordfish steaks. Sprinkle with lemon juice and garlic powder. Cover with wax paper. Microwave at 70% (Medium High) for 5 to 6 minutes, or until fish flakes with fork, re-arranging once. Serve each steak topped with about ¼ cup sauce. Sprinkle each with 1 teaspoon toasted coconut.

Per Serving:			
Calories:	170	Cholesterol:	29 mg.
Protein:	16 g.	Sodium:	166 mg.
Carbohydrate:	19 g.	Fiber:	2 g.
Fat (total):	4 g.	Exchanges:	2 lean meat, 1 vegetable, 1 fruit
Saturated Fat:	1 g.		

Tropical Sweet & Sour Swordfish

Rice Pilaf   *Fresh Broccoli Flowerets*

Orange Roughy with ▶ Kiwi-Orange Sauce

Sauce:

¾ teaspoon cornstarch
⅓ cup orange juice
4 kiwifruit, peeled and sliced (24 slices), divided
2 teaspoons olive oil
1 teaspoon white wine vinegar

18 oz. orange roughy fillets, cut into 6 serving-size pieces
¼ cup orange juice
½ teaspoon grated orange peel
6 orange slices

6 servings

In 2-cup measure, place cornstarch. Blend in ⅓ cup orange juice. Microwave at High for 1½ to 2 minutes, or until mixture is thickened and translucent, stirring once. Set aside.

In food processor or blender, place 12 kiwi slices, the oil and vinegar. Process until smooth. Pour into thickened orange juice mixture. Mix well. Set aside.

In 10-inch square casserole, arrange orange roughy fillets in single layer. In 1-cup measure, combine ¼ cup orange juice and the orange peel. Pour over fillets. Cover with wax paper. Microwave at High for 6 to 10 minutes, or until fish flakes with fork. Top each serving with 3 tablespoons sauce. Garnish with remaining kiwi slices and the orange slices.

Per Serving:	
Calories:	171
Protein:	13 g.
Carbohydrate:	12 g.
Fat (total):	8 g.
Saturated Fat:	—
Cholesterol:	17 mg.
Sodium:	56 mg.
Fiber:	2 g.
Exchanges:	2 lean meat, 1 fruit

Orange Roughy with Kiwi-Orange Sauce

Steamed Asparagus

Broiled Tuna Steaks with Kiwi-Papaya Salsa

¾ cup chopped red pepper
½ cup chopped red onion
1 tablespoon finely chopped fresh or canned jalapeño pepper
½ teaspoon grated lime peel
1 tablespoon plus 1 teaspoon lime juice, divided
2 teaspoons olive oil
¼ teaspoon cumin seed, crushed

½ cup peeled and cubed papaya (¼-inch cubes)
1 kiwifruit, peeled and cubed (¼-inch cubes)
1 tuna steak (12 oz.), about ½-inch thick, cut into 4 serving-size pieces
Nonstick vegetable cooking spray

4 servings

In 1-quart casserole, combine red pepper, onion, jalapeño pepper, lime peel, 1 teaspoon lime juice, the oil and cumin seed. Cover. Microwave at High for 4 to 5 minutes, or until vegetables are tender, stirring once. Add papaya and kiwi. Mix well. Re-cover. Chill at least 1 hour.

In 8-inch square baking dish, place tuna steak pieces. Brush evenly with remaining 1 tablespoon lime juice.

Spray conventional broiler pan with nonstick vegetable cooking spray. Arrange tuna steaks on prepared broiler pan. Place under conventional broiler, 4 inches from heat. Broil for 3 to 5 minutes, or until tuna flakes with fork. Serve tuna steaks topped with about ⅓ cup salsa.

Per Serving:			
Calories:	148	Cholesterol:	28 mg.
Protein:	18 g.	Sodium:	63 mg.
Carbohydrate:	8 g.	Fiber:	2 g.
Fat (total):	5 g.	Exchanges:	2½ lean meat, ½ fruit
Saturated Fat:	1 g.		

Broiled Tuna Steaks with Kiwi-Papaya Salsa

Saffron Rice

Japanese Marinated Salmon Fillets

12-oz. salmon fillet, cut into 4
 serving-size pieces

Marinade:

 2 tablespoons low-sodium soy
 sauce
 1 tablespoon lemon juice
 1 tablespoon packed brown
 sugar
 1 clove garlic

 1 leek (6 oz.), trimmed, cut in
 half lengthwise, rinsed,
 thinly sliced
 ½ cup julienne carrot
 (1½ × ⅛-inch strips)

4 servings

Arrange salmon fillets skin-sides-up in 8-inch square baking dish. Set aside.

In small mixing bowl, combine marinade ingredients. Stir to dissolve sugar. Pour mixture over fillets, turning fillets to coat sides. Cover with plastic wrap. Chill for 1 hour.

Turn fillets skin-sides-down. Sprinkle with leek and carrot. Re-cover with plastic wrap. Microwave at 70% (Medium High) for 8 to 9 minutes, or until fish flakes easily with fork, rearranging pieces twice. Serve with vegetables.

Per Serving:	
Calories:	196
Protein:	20 g.
Carbohydrate:	12 g.
Fat (total):	7 g.
Saturated Fat:	1 g.
Cholesterol:	53 mg.
Sodium:	374 mg.
Fiber:	1 g.
Exchanges:	2½ lean meat, 1 vegetable, ½ fruit

Japanese Marinated Salmon Fillets

*Cold Lemon Cucumber Soup
(page 40)
Brown Rice*

Mint-Raspberry Salmon Fillets

 ¼ cup chopped fresh mint
 leaves
 2 tablespoons raspberry
 vinegar

 2 tablespoons olive oil
 1 tablespoon honey
12-oz. salmon fillet, cut into
 4 serving-size pieces

4 servings

In 2-cup measure, combine all ingredients, except salmon. Microwave at High for 1 to 1¼ minutes, or just until mixture begins to boil, stirring once. Pour mixture into 8-inch square baking dish.

Arrange salmon fillets skin-sides-up in dish, turning to coat sides with mint mixture. Cover with plastic wrap. Chill 30 minutes.

Turn salmon fillets skin-sides-down. Re-cover. Microwave at 70% (Medium High) for 6 to 8 minutes, or until fish flakes easily with fork. Discard cooking liquid. Serve hot or chilled.

Per Serving:		Cholesterol:	53 mg.
Calories:	162		
Protein:	18 g.	Sodium:	40 mg.
Carbohydrate:	1 g.	Fiber:	—
Fat (total):	9 g.	Exchanges:	2½ lean meat, ½ fat
Saturated Fat:	2 g.		

Mint-Raspberry Salmon Fillets

Bibb Lettuce Salad   *Sweet Corn*

Cold Poached Salmon with Lemon-Chive Sauce

Sauce:
- ¼ cup lemon-flavored low-fat yogurt
- 2 tablespoons sour cream dairy blend
- 2 teaspoons snipped fresh chives
- ¼ teaspoon sugar
- ⅛ teaspoon salt

Poaching Liquid:
- 1¾ cups Low-fat Chicken Broth (page 36) or defatted chicken broth
- 2 medium carrots, sliced (¼-inch slices)
- ¼ cup sliced green onions
- 1 teaspoon grated lemon peel
- 4 thin lemon slices
- ¼ teaspoon pepper

- 6 salmon steaks (4 oz. each)

6 servings

Per Serving:	
Calories:	185
Protein:	22 g.
Carbohydrate:	3 g.
Fat (total):	9 g.
Saturated Fat:	2 g.
Cholesterol:	63 mg.
Sodium:	113 mg.
Fiber:	—
Exchanges:	3 lean meat, ½ vegetable

Cold Poached Salmon with Lemon-Chive Sauce

Asparagus Bundles (page 127)

How to Microwave Cold Poached Salmon with Lemon-Chive Sauce

Combine sauce ingredients in small mixing bowl. Mix well. Cover. Chill at least 4 hours or overnight. In 10-inch square casserole, combine all poaching liquid ingredients. Mix well. Cover. Microwave at High for 8 to 11 minutes, or until mixture begins to boil.

Place salmon in liquid with meaty portions toward outside edges. Re-cover. Microwave at 70% (Medium High) for 9 to 12 minutes, or until fish flakes easily with fork, rotating dish 2 or 3 times.

Chill salmon and poaching liquid at least 4 hours, or until cold. Just before serving, remove salmon from liquid. Discard liquid. Spoon about 1 heaping tablespoon sauce over each serving.

Halibut with Creole Relish ▲

¼	cup chopped celery		¼	teaspoon dried basil leaves
¼	cup chopped green pepper		¼	teaspoon dried thyme leaves
¼	cup chopped onion		¼	teaspoon sugar
1	tablespoon plus 1 teaspoon lemon juice, divided		⅛	teaspoon salt
1	teaspoon vegetable oil		3	to 5 drops red pepper sauce
1	clove garlic, minced		½	cup seeded chopped tomato
½	teaspoon dried oregano leaves		2	halibut steaks (8 oz. each), about 1 inch thick

4 servings

In 1-quart casserole, combine celery, pepper, onion, 1 teaspoon lemon juice, the oil, garlic, oregano, basil, thyme, sugar, salt and pepper sauce. Mix well. Cover. Microwave at High for 3 to 4 minutes, or until vegetables are tender, stirring once. Stir in tomato. Set aside.

Cut bone from center of each halibut steak, using thin blade of knife and being careful not to slice all the way through ends of steaks. Cut each steak in half crosswise to yield 4 serving-size pieces.

In 8-inch square baking dish or on microwave roasting rack, arrange halibut steaks. Sprinkle with remaining 1 tablespoon lemon juice. Cover with wax paper. Microwave at 70% (Medium High) for 5 to 7 minutes, or until fish flakes easily with fork, rotating dish once or twice. Serve each halibut steak topped with about 3 tablespoons relish.

Per Serving:			
Calories:	140	Cholesterol:	32 mg.
Protein:	21 g.	Sodium:	133 mg.
Carbohydrate:	5 g.	Fiber:	1 g.
Fat (total):	4 g.	Exchanges:	2½ lean meat, 1 vegetable
Saturated Fat:	1 g.		

Fresh Catch with Yogurt Tartar Sauce

⅓	cup plain low-fat or nonfat yogurt
2	tablespoons reduced-calorie mayonnaise
2	tablespoons pickle relish
12	oz. walleye fillets, about ½ inch thick, cut into 4 serving-size pieces
1	teaspoon grated lemon peel Paprika

4 servings

In small bowl, combine yogurt, mayonnaise and relish. Mix well. Set aside.

In 8-inch square baking dish, place walleye fillets. Sprinkle with grated lemon peel and paprika. Cover with wax paper.

Microwave at High for 3 to 5 minutes, or until fish flakes easily with fork. Serve each walleye fillet topped with about 2 tablespoons sauce.

Per Serving:	
Calories:	122
Protein:	17 g.
Carbohydrate:	5 g.
Fat (total):	3 g.
Saturated Fat:	1 g.
Cholesterol:	77 mg.
Sodium:	155 mg.
Fiber:	—
Exchanges:	½ skim milk, 2 lean meat

Halibut with Creole Relish

Southern-style Succotash (page 136)
Corn Bread

Fresh Catch with Yogurt Tartar Sauce

Steamed Fresh Broccoli Spears

Shrimp & Basil Pizza

Nonstick vegetable cooking spray
1 pkg. (16 oz.) hot roll mix
1 teaspoon dried basil leaves
½ teaspoon garlic powder
1¼ cups hot tap water
2 tablespoons olive oil

Topping:

12 oz. medium shrimp, shelled and deveined
1 cup seeded chopped tomato
¼ cup chopped red onion
2 tablespoons shredded fresh basil leaves (optional)
1 tablespoon olive oil
2 teaspoons white wine vinegar
¼ teaspoon sugar
1 cup shredded hard farmer cheese (4 oz.)

6 servings

NOTE: Recipe not recommended for ovens with less than 600 cooking watts.

Heat conventional oven to 400°F. Spray two 12-inch pizza pans with nonstick vegetable cooking spray. Set aside.

In large mixing bowl, combine hot roll mix, dried basil leaves and garlic powder. Add hot water and 2 tablespoons oil. Stir until particles are moistened. Knead dough on lightly floured surface for 5 minutes. Divide in half. Pat into prepared pans. Prick thoroughly with fork. Cover and let rise for 15 minutes.

Bake crusts 12 to 15 minutes, or until deep golden brown. Remove crusts to wire cooling racks. Wrap one crust in foil and freeze for future use. Place remaining crust on 12-inch glass platter. Set aside.

In 9-inch cake dish, arrange shrimp in single layer. Cover with plastic wrap. Microwave at 70% (Medium High) for 3 to 5 minutes, or until shrimp are firm and opaque, stirring once. Drain. Add remaining ingredients, except cheese. Mix well.

Sprinkle crust evenly with cheese. Top evenly with shrimp mixture. Microwave pizza at 50% (Medium) for 4 to 6 minutes, or until cheese is melted and crust is warm, rotating platter once.

Per Serving:			
Calories:	300	Cholesterol:	82 mg.
Protein:	18 g.	Sodium:	411 mg.
Carbohydrate:	32 g.	Fiber:	2 g.
Fat (total):	11 g.	Exchanges:	1½ starch, 1½ lean meat,
Saturated Fat:	4 g.		2 vegetable, 1 fat

Shrimp & Basil Pizza

Tossed Green Salad

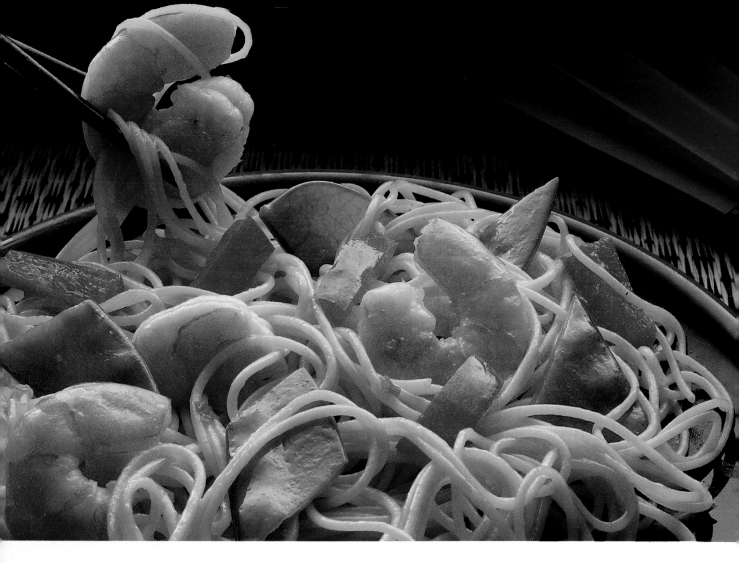

Szechuan Shrimp

6 oz. uncooked capellini
   (angel hair spaghetti)
1 lb. medium shrimp, shelled
   and deveined
2 teaspoons cornstarch
1 teaspoon sugar
1 clove garlic, minced
½ teaspoon low-sodium instant
   chicken bouillon granules
⅛ to ¼ teaspoon crushed red
   pepper flakes
   Dash to ⅛ teaspoon white
   pepper
⅓ cup water
3 tablespoons low-sodium soy
   sauce
2 teaspoons sesame oil
1½ teaspoons white wine
   vinegar
1 cup red pepper strips
   (1 × ¼-inch)
1 cup pea pods, cut into thirds

6 servings

Prepare capellini as directed on package. Rinse and drain. Set aside. In 10-inch square casserole, place shrimp. Cover. Microwave at 70% (Medium High) for 5 to 8 minutes, or until shrimp are firm and opaque, stirring once. Drain. Set aside.

In 2-quart casserole, combine cornstarch, sugar, garlic, bouillon, red pepper flakes and pepper. Blend in water, soy sauce, oil and vinegar.

Add pepper strips and pea pods. Mix well. Microwave at High for 5 to 6 minutes, or until vegetables are tender-crisp and sauce is thickened and translucent, stirring twice.

Add cooked capellini and the shrimp to vegetable mixture. Toss to coat. Microwave at High for 2 to 3 minutes, or until hot.

Per Serving:			
Calories:	205	Cholesterol:	86 mg.
Protein:	17 g.	Sodium:	406 mg.
Carbohydrate:	27 g.	Fiber:	2 g.
Fat (total):	3 g.	Exchanges:	1 starch, 1½ lean meat, 2 vegetable
Saturated Fat:	—		

Szechuan Shrimp

Cardamom Orange Spinach Salad (page 47)

Cajun Skewered Shrimp ▶

1	tablespoon plus 2 teaspoons olive oil	½	teaspoon dried thyme leaves
1	clove garlic, minced	⅛	teaspoon cayenne
½	teaspoon ground cumin	⅛	teaspoon pepper
½	teaspoon dried oregano leaves	12	large shrimp (1 oz. each), shelled and deveined
½	teaspoon paprika	4	wooden skewers, 8-inch

4 servings

In medium mixing bowl, combine all ingredients, except shrimp. Mix well. Add shrimp. Toss to coat. Cover with plastic wrap. Chill 1 hour. On each skewer, thread 3 shrimp. Arrange skewered shrimp in single layer on microwave roasting rack or in 8-inch square baking dish. Cover with wax paper. Microwave at 70% (Medium High) for 2 to 4 minutes, or until shrimp are firm and opaque, rearranging once.

Per Serving:

Calories:	122	Cholesterol:	97 mg.
Protein:	13 g.	Sodium:	95 mg.
Carbohydrate:	1 g.	Fiber:	—
Fat (total):	7 g.	Exchanges:	2 lean meat
Saturated Fat:	1 g.		

Cajun Skewered Shrimp

Rice Pilaf   *Red, Green and Yellow Pepper Salad*

Shrimp Jambalaya

2	cups Low-fat Chicken Broth (page 36) or defatted chicken broth	1	pkg. (9 oz.) frozen artichoke hearts
1	cup uncooked long-grain white rice	¼	cup snipped fresh parsley
1	cup red pepper chunks (1-inch chunks)	1	teaspoon chili powder
1	cup green pepper chunks (1-inch chunks)	1	clove garlic, minced
		¼	teaspoon paprika
		¼	teaspoon salt
		12	oz. medium shrimp, shelled and deveined

6 servings

In 3-quart casserole, combine all ingredients, except shrimp. Mix well. Cover. Microwave at High for 5 minutes. Microwave at 50% (Medium) for 40 to 45 minutes longer, or until rice is tender and liquid is absorbed, stirring twice. Stir in shrimp. Re-cover. Microwave at 50% (Medium) for 4 to 5 minutes, or until shrimp are firm and opaque, stirring once.

Per Serving:

Calories:	185	Cholesterol:	65 mg.
Protein:	12 g.	Sodium:	219 mg.
Carbohydrate:	31 g.	Fiber:	3 g.
Fat (total):	1 g.	Exchanges:	1 starch, 1 lean meat, 3 vegetable
Saturated Fat:	—		

Shrimp Jambalaya

Sautéed Zucchini and Yellow Summer Squash Strips

Jumbo Crab & Cheese-stuffed Mushrooms

12 large fresh mushrooms (2 to
    2½-inch diameter)
 1 tablespoon snipped fresh
    parsley
 1 tablespoon margarine
 1 tablespoon sherry
 1 clove garlic, minced
 ¼ teaspoon dried thyme leaves
 ¼ teaspoon salt
 1 cup cooked flaked crab meat
 ½ cup shredded hard farmer
    cheese (2 oz.)
 1 slice soft whole wheat bread,
    crumbled (½ cup)

Sauce:
 ¼ cup nonfat dry milk powder
 2 teaspoons all-purpose flour
 ⅛ teaspoon salt
 ½ cup water
 1 tablespoon sherry
 ¼ cup shredded hard farmer
    cheese (1 oz.)

4 servings

Remove stems from mushrooms. Set caps aside. Finely chop stems (about 1 cup chopped). Place chopped stems in 2-quart casserole.

Add parsley, margarine, 1 tablespoon sherry, the garlic, thyme and ¼ teaspoon salt. Cover. Microwave at High for 3 to 4 minutes, or until margarine is melted and mushrooms are tender, stirring once. Stir in crab meat, ½ cup cheese and the bread crumbs. Mix well.

Arrange mushroom caps in 8-inch square baking dish. Stuff each cap with 2 scant tablespoons of mixture. Cover with plastic wrap. Microwave at 70% (Medium High) for 8 to 9 minutes, or until mushrooms are tender and filling is hot, rotating dish once or twice. Let stand, covered, while preparing sauce.

In 2-cup measure, combine milk powder, flour and ⅛ teaspoon salt. Blend in water and 1 tablespoon sherry. Microwave at High for 2 to 2½ minutes, or until mixture thickens and bubbles, stirring twice.

Add ¼ cup cheese. Stir until melted. Place 3 stuffed mushrooms on each plate. Top with 2 tablespoons sauce. Garnish with parsley, if desired.

Per Serving:			
Calories:	204	Cholesterol:	38 mg.
Protein:	16 g.	Sodium:	733 mg.
Carbohydrate:	12 g.	Fiber:	1 g.
Fat (total):	10 g.	Exchanges:	1½ lean meat, 1 vegetable, ½ skim
Saturated Fat:	5 g.		milk, 1 fat

Jumbo Crab & Cheese-stuffed Mushrooms

Raspberry Fruit Dip (page 20)   *Steamed Carrots*

Linguine & Red Clam Sauce

8 oz. uncooked linguine
1 zucchini (4 oz.), cut in half lengthwise and thinly sliced (1 cup)
½ cup chopped carrot
⅓ cup chopped celery
2 cloves garlic, minced
2 teaspoons olive oil
½ teaspoon dried marjoram leaves
¼ teaspoon salt
¼ teaspoon pepper
¼ teaspoon sugar
1 can (16 oz.) whole tomatoes, cut up and undrained
1 can (6½ oz.) chopped clams, undrained
2 tablespoons tomato paste

4 servings

Prepare linguine as directed on package. Rinse and drain. Cover to keep warm. Set aside.

In 2-quart casserole, combine zucchini, carrot, celery, garlic, oil and seasonings. Mix well. Cover. Microwave at High for 5½ to 8 minutes, or until vegetables are tender, stirring once or twice.

Add remaining ingredients. Mix well. Microwave at High, uncovered, for 5 to 9 minutes, or until flavors are blended and sauce is hot. Serve sauce over linguine.

Per Serving:	
Calories:	342
Protein:	21 g.
Carbohydrate:	55 g.
Fat (total):	4 g.
Saturated Fat:	—
Cholesterol:	31 mg.
Sodium:	443 mg.
Fiber:	4 g.
Exchanges:	2½ starch, 1 lean meat, 3½ vegetable

Linguine & Red Clam Sauce

Tossed Green Salad
Garlic Bread

Cumin Citrus Scallops ▲

4 oz. uncooked spinach fettucini
2 tablespoons plus 2 teaspoons olive oil, divided
1 tablespoon snipped fresh cilantro (optional)
1 medium orange
1 tablespoon lime zest
2 teaspoons margarine
1 clove garlic, minced
½ teaspoon ground cumin
¼ teaspoon salt
¼ teaspoon freshly ground pepper
1 lb. bay scallops

4 servings

Prepare fettucini as directed on package. Rinse and drain. Toss with 2 teaspoons oil and the cilantro. Cover to keep warm. Set aside.

Using sharp knife, cut peel and white membrane from orange. Slice orange crosswise into ¼-inch slices. Quarter each slice. Set aside.

In 2-quart casserole, combine the remaining 2 tablespoons oil, the lime zest, margarine, garlic, cumin, salt and pepper. Cover. Microwave at High for 1½ to 2 minutes, or until margarine is melted and garlic softens, stirring once.

Add scallops. Toss to coat. Re-cover. Microwave at 70% (Medium High) for 5 to 7 minutes, or until scallops are firm and opaque, stirring twice.

Add orange pieces. Toss to combine. Serve scallops over cooked spinach fettucini.

Per Serving:			
Calories:	319	Cholesterol:	37 mg.
Protein:	23 g.	Sodium:	332 mg.
Carbohydrate:	29 g.	Fiber:	2 g.
Fat (total):	12 g.	Exchanges:	2 starch, 2 lean meat, 1 fat
Saturated Fat:	2 g.		

Cumin Citrus Scallops

Tossed Green Salad   *Hard Rolls*

Poultry

Properly prepared, turkey and chicken are excellent sources of high-quality, low-fat protein. To make poultry low-fat, it must be skinned. A 3½-ounce serving of roasted, skin-on white meat chicken contains 10.9 grams of fat; removing the skin removes more than half the fat, leaving a total of 4.5 grams. When you skin poultry, trim the chunks of visible fat as well.

If you bone poultry before cooking, save the bones and scraps. Collect them in the freezer in a heavy plastic bag until you have enough to make Low-fat Chicken Broth (page 36).

The microwave oven cooks skinned poultry juicy and tender. With most conventional methods, skinned poultry dries out and sticks to the pan.

Fresh turkey breast slices, tenderloins and 85% lean ground turkey are ready to microwave. To reduce fat, skin bone-in and boneless rolled turkey breasts, or ask your butcher to prepare a skin-free, boneless rolled breast.

Microwave skinned turkey or chicken breasts for sandwich meat. It contains less sodium than deli products, and costs less, too.

The following chart compares the saturated fat, cholesterol and total fat content of *skinned* turkey and chicken, ranking them from lower to higher saturated fat in each category. (Portions evaluated were larger than those recommended by the American Heart Association.) No figures are available for Cornish game hens. Duck, goose, turkey bologna and chicken and turkey frankfurters contain over 15 grams of fat, and are omitted.

Fats & Cholesterol Comparison of Skinned Poultry

Product (3½ ounces, cooked)	Saturated Fatty Acids (grams)	Cholesterol (milligrams)	Total Fat (grams)
Turkey			
fryer-roaster, light meat	0.4	86	1.9
fryer-roaster, dark meat	1.4	112	4.3
roll, light and dark meat	2.0	55	7.0
Chicken			
broiler-fryer, light meat	1.3	85	4.5
broiler-fryer, dark meat	2.4	77	9.7

Source: United States Department of Agriculture, Science and Education Administration Agriculture Handbook 8-5. 1979.

How to Bone a Half Chicken Breast

Skin breast with fingers. Using a boning knife, cut against breastbone to loosen meat.

Angle sharp edge of knife toward bone. Cut against ribs and wishbone, pulling meat from bones as you cut.

Scrape and pull out tendon on underside of meat. Check with fingers for pieces of wishbone that may remain. Freeze the bones for broth (page 35).

Turkey Salad in Phyllo Bowls

Nonstick vegetable cooking
   spray
½ lb. uncooked turkey breast
   slices, cut into 1-inch pieces
1 Rome apple (8 oz.), cored
   and cubed (½-inch cubes)
½ cup sliced celery
½ cup seedless green grapes
½ cup seedless red grapes
¼ cup chopped red onion
⅓ cup plain low-fat or nonfat
   yogurt

2 tablespoons reduced-calorie
   mayonnaise
¼ teaspoon ground cinnamon
⅛ teaspoon salt
2 tablespoons margarine or
   butter
4 sheets frozen phyllo dough
   (18 × 14-inch sheets),
   defrosted
   Leaf lettuce

4 servings

Per Serving:			
Calories:	244	Cholesterol:	36 mg.
Protein:	15 g.	Sodium:	290 mg.
Carbohydrate:	22 g.	Fiber:	3 g.
Fat (total):	11 g.	Exchanges:	2 lean meat, 1 vegetable, 1 fruit,
Saturated Fat:	2 g.		1 fat

Turkey Salad in Phyllo Bowls

Tangy Vegetable Dip (page 21)   ·   *Iced Tea*

How to Make Turkey Salad in Phyllo Bowls

Heat conventional oven to 375°F.
On large cookie sheet with sides,
place four 10-ounce custard cups
upside down, spacing cups at
least 3 inches apart. Spray bot-
toms and sides of cups with nonstick vegetable cooking spray.
Set aside.

Place turkey in 2-quart casserole. Cover. Microwave at High
for 4 to 5 minutes, or until turkey
is no longer pink, stirring twice.
Drain. In medium mixing bowl,
combine turkey, apple, celery,
grapes, onion, yogurt, mayonnaise, cinnamon and salt. Mix
well. Cover and chill.

Place margarine in small bowl.
Microwave at High for 45 seconds to 1 minute, or until melted.
Place two 20 × 12-inch pieces of
plastic wrap side by side lengthwise on flat work surface.

Lay 1 phyllo sheet on plastic-wrap-covered work surface. Brush lightly with one-fourth of melted margarine. Lay another sheet over first and brush lightly with one-third of remaining margarine. With scissors, cut sheets into 4 equal-size pieces, each approximately 8½ × 7 inches.

Drape 1 piece of phyllo buttered-side-up over each custard cup. Press gently to form around cup. Repeat with remaining 2 phyllo sheets. Bake for 10 to 15 minutes, or until golden brown. Cool completely.

Lift phyllo bowls carefully off custard cups. Line each with leaf lettuce. Divide salad evenly among phyllo bowls.

Cider-sauced Turkey Breast

1 tablespoon all-purpose flour
3-lb. boneless, skinless whole
   turkey breast*
1 medium onion, cut into 8
   wedges
1½ cups apple cider, divided
¼ teaspoon ground cardamom
¼ teaspoon salt
1 tablespoon packed brown
   sugar
2 teaspoons cornstarch
¼ teaspoon ground cinnamon
2 Rome apples (8 oz. each),
   sliced crosswise into ¼-
   inch rounds, seeds
   removed

16 servings

Place flour in large oven cooking bag. Hold bag closed at top and shake to coat. Add turkey breast and onion to bag. In 1-cup measure, combine ½ cup cider, the cardamom and salt. Mix well. Pour over turkey breast and onion. Secure bag with nylon tie. Make six ½-inch slits in neck of bag below tie.

Place bag in 8-inch square baking dish. Microwave at High for 5 minutes. Microwave at 50% (Medium) for 32 to 55 minutes longer, or until internal temperature registers 170°F in several places, turning once. Let stand in bag for 10 minutes.

In 2-quart casserole, combine sugar, cornstarch and cinnamon. Blend in remaining 1 cup cider. Add apples. Stir gently to coat. Cover. Microwave at High for 6 to 11 minutes, or until sauce is thickened and translucent and apples are tender, stirring twice. Serve turkey with apples and sauce.

*Ask your butcher to prepare a skinless turkey breast.

Per Serving:			
Calories:	104	Cholesterol:	32 mg.
Protein:	13 g.	Sodium:	64 mg.
Carbohydrate:	8 g.	Fiber:	1 g.
Fat (total):	2 g.	Exchanges:	1½ lean meat, ½ fruit
Saturated Fat:	1 g.		

Cider-sauced Turkey Breast

Saffron Squash & Leek Soup (page 41)
Wild Rice

Teriyaki Turkey with Pineapple Rice

1 can (8 oz.) pineapple tidbits
   in juice
⅔ cup uncooked long-grain
   white rice
¼ teaspoon salt
2 tablespoons packed brown
   sugar
1 tablespoon cornstarch
½ teaspoon ground ginger
1 clove garlic, minced
¼ cup low-sodium soy sauce
2 tablespoons sherry
1 tablespoon vegetable oil
¾ lb. uncooked turkey breast
   slices, cut into thin strips
1 cup julienne carrots
   (2 × ¼-inch strips)
1 cup green pepper chunks
   (1-inch chunks)
2 tablespoons water
1 medium tomato, seeded and
   cut into 1-inch chunks

4 servings

Drain pineapple juice into 2-cup measure. Add hot water to equal 2 cups. In 2-quart casserole, combine pineapple, juice mixture, rice and salt. Cover. Microwave at High for 5 minutes. Microwave at 50% (Medium) for 15 to 18 minutes longer, or until rice is tender and liquid is absorbed. Let stand, covered, for 5 minutes. Stir with fork to fluff rice. Re-cover. Set aside.

In 2-quart casserole, combine brown sugar, cornstarch, ginger and garlic. Blend in soy sauce, sherry and oil. Add turkey. Toss to coat. Cover. Microwave at High for 5 to 9 minutes, or until turkey is no longer pink, stirring twice. Set aside.

In 1-quart casserole, place carrots, green pepper and 2 tablespoons water. Cover. Microwave at High for 4 to 6 minutes, or until vegetables are tender-crisp, stirring once. Drain. Add cooked vegetables and tomato to turkey and sauce. Mix well. Cover. Microwave at High for 2 to 3 minutes, or until hot, stirring once. Microwave rice at High for 2 to 3 minutes, or until hot, stirring once. Serve turkey mixture over rice.

Per Serving:			
Calories:	345	Cholesterol:	53 mg.
Protein:	24 g.	Sodium:	822 mg.
Carbohydrate:	50 g.	Fiber:	3 g.
Fat (total):	4 g.	Exchanges:	1½ starch, 2 lean meat,
Saturated Fat:	1 g.		1 vegetable, 1½ fruit

Teriyaki Turkey with Pineapple Rice

Hot Tea   *Fortune Cookies*

Hungarian Chicken Breasts

3 boneless whole chicken
   breasts (8 to 10 oz. each),
   split in half, skin removed
1¾ teaspoons paprika, divided
⅛ teaspoon garlic powder
1 small onion, thinly sliced
2 teaspoons all-purpose flour
½ teaspoon instant chicken
   bouillon granules
⅛ teaspoon pepper
¾ cup evaporated skim milk
1 tablespoon white wine
2 tablespoons sour cream
   dairy blend
3 cups hot cooked rice
2 tablespoons snipped fresh
   parsley

6 servings

In 8-inch square baking dish, arrange chicken breast halves in single layer. Sprinkle with ¼ teaspoon paprika and the garlic powder. Top with onions. Cover with wax paper. Microwave at High for 7½ to 12 minutes, or until chicken is no longer pink and juices run clear, rearranging twice. Set aside, covered.

In 4-cup measure, combine flour, the remaining 1½ teaspoons paprika, the bouillon and pepper. Blend in milk and wine. Microwave at High for 2½ to 4 minutes, or until mixture thickens and bubbles, stirring 2 or 3 times with whisk.

Add sour cream dairy blend. Mix well. Serve chicken with rice. Top each serving with 2½ tablespoons sauce. Garnish each serving evenly with parsley.

Per Serving:			
Calories:	294	Cholesterol:	74 mg.
Protein:	31 g.	Sodium:	137 mg.
Carbohydrate:	31 g.	Fiber:	1 g.
Fat (total):	4 g.	Exchanges:	1½ starch, 3 lean meat,
Saturated Fat:	1 g.		½ vegetable, ½ skim milk

Hungarian Chicken Breasts

Whole Green Beans

Creamy Chicken & Vegetable Casserole

6 oz. uncooked rotini pasta (about 2¼ cups)
1 boneless whole chicken breast (8 to 10 oz.), split in half, skin removed
2 cups thinly sliced zucchini (about 9 oz.)
1 cup julienne carrot (1½ × ¼-inch strips)
1 cup fresh mushrooms, quartered
2 tablespoons snipped fresh parsley
½ teaspoon dried marjoram leaves
⅛ teaspoon garlic powder
⅔ cup nonfat dry milk powder
2 tablespoons all-purpose flour
1 teaspoon instant chicken bouillon granules
⅛ teaspoon salt
1 cup water
¼ cup white wine
1 teaspoon margarine

6 servings

Prepare pasta as directed on package. Rinse and drain. Set aside. Cut each chicken breast half crosswise into 1-inch strips. Set aside.

In 2-quart casserole, combine vegetables and seasonings. Add chicken pieces. Cover. Microwave at High for 6 to 8 minutes, or until chicken is no longer pink, stirring once or twice. Add cooked pasta. Re-cover. Set aside.

In 4-cup measure, combine milk powder, flour, bouillon and salt. Blend in water and wine. Add margarine. Microwave at High for 3½ to 7 minutes, or until mixture thickens and bubbles, stirring with whisk after first minute and then every 2 minutes.

Pour sauce over chicken and vegetable mixture. Toss to coat. Cover. Microwave at High for 2 to 4 minutes, or until hot.

Per Serving:			
Calories:	235	Cholesterol:	26 mg.
Protein:	18 g.	Sodium:	208 mg.
Carbohydrate:	34 g.	Fiber:	2 g.
Fat (total):	2 g.	Exchanges:	1½ starch, 1 lean meat, 2 vegetable
Saturated Fat:	—		

Creamy Chicken & Vegetable Casserole

Tossed Green Salad with Sweet Apple & Poppy Seed Dressing (page 45)

Barbecued Chicken Sandwich

1 boneless whole chicken
  breast (8 to 10 oz.), skin
  removed
1 small onion, sliced
  (about ½ cup)
¼ cup chopped green pepper
1 clove garlic, minced
1 teaspoon olive oil
1 can (8 oz.) tomato sauce
3 tablespoons tomato paste
2 tablespoons packed brown
  sugar
1 tablespoon red wine vinegar
1 tablespoon Worcestershire
  sauce
½ teaspoon dry mustard
4 drops red pepper sauce
4 whole wheat hamburger buns

4 servings

On roasting rack or in 8-inch square baking dish, place chicken breast. Cover with wax paper. Microwave at High for 3 to 4 minutes, or until no longer pink and juices run clear, rotating once. Set aside.

In 2-quart casserole, combine onion, pepper, garlic and oil. Cover. Microwave at High for 2 to 3 minutes, or until vegetables are tender, stirring once.

Add remaining ingredients, except chicken and buns. Mix well. Microwave at High, uncovered, for 4 to 5 minutes, or until slightly thickened and flavors are blended, stirring once.

Shred chicken and add to barbecue sauce. Cover. Microwave at High for 1½ to 2 minutes, or until hot, stirring once. Spoon ½ cup mixture onto each bun.

Per Serving:			
Calories:	245	Cholesterol:	37 mg.
Protein:	19 g.	Sodium:	727 mg.
Carbohydrate:	35 g.	Fiber:	3 g.
Fat (total):	4 g.	Exchanges:	2 starch, 1½ lean meat, 1 vegetable
Saturated Fat:	1 g.		

Barbecued Chicken Sandwich

Lemon Broccoli & Cauliflower Salad (page 46)   *Orange Mineral Water*

Peach & Chicken Almond Ding

- 3 cups unsweetened frozen sliced peaches
- 1 tablespoon cornstarch
- 1 teaspoon sugar
- ¼ teaspoon ground ginger
- ⅛ teaspoon white pepper
- 1 clove garlic, minced
- ¼ cup low-sodium soy sauce
- 2 tablespoons white wine
- 1 teaspoon vegetable oil
- 1 boneless whole chicken breast (8 to 10 oz.), skin removed, cut into 1-inch pieces
- 2 cups fresh pea pods, sliced diagonally into thirds
- 1 cup sliced bok choy
- 2 tablespoons whole almonds
- 2 cups hot cooked rice

4 servings

In 1-quart casserole, place peaches. Cover. Microwave at High for 4 to 5 minutes, or until peaches are defrosted, stirring once. Drain. Set aside.

In 2-quart casserole, combine cornstarch, sugar, ginger, pepper and garlic. Blend in soy sauce, wine and oil. Add chicken. Stir to coat. Cover.

Microwave at High for 5 to 8 minutes, or until chicken is no longer pink, stirring 2 or 3 times. Add peaches, pea pods, bok choy and almonds to chicken. Mix well. Re-cover. Microwave at High for 2 to 4 minutes, or until hot. Serve over rice.

Per Serving:
Calories:	326
Protein:	20 g.
Carbohydrate:	49 g.
Fat (total):	5 g.
Saturated Fat:	1 g.
Cholesterol:	36 mg.
Sodium:	681 mg.
Fiber:	7 g.
Exchanges:	2 starch, 1½ lean meat, 1 vegetable, 1 fruit

Peach & Chicken Almond Ding

Spiced Shrimp Spring Rolls (page 28)

Lemon Thyme Chicken with Vegetables

1 cup julienne green pepper
   (2 × ¼-inch strips)
1 cup julienne red pepper
   (2 × ¼-inch strips)
1 cup julienne zucchini
   (2 × ¼-inch strips)
1 cup frozen peas
½ cup thinly sliced carrot
2 bone-in whole chicken
   breasts (10 to 12 oz. each),
   split in half, skin removed
2 tablespoons fresh lemon juice
1 teaspoon grated lemon peel
¾ teaspoon dried thyme leaves
¼ teaspoon salt
¼ teaspoon pepper

4 servings

In 8-inch square baking dish, place peppers, zucchini, peas and carrot. Arrange chicken breast halves over vegetables with thickest portions toward outside edges. Sprinkle evenly with lemon juice.

In small bowl, combine lemon peel, thyme, salt and pepper. Mix well. Sprinkle evenly over chicken breasts and vegetables. Cover with plastic wrap. Microwave at High for 10 to 12 minutes, or until chicken near bone is no longer pink and juices run clear, rearranging chicken once.

Per Serving:	
Calories:	203
Protein:	29 g.
Carbohydrate:	13 g.
Fat (total):	4 g.
Saturated Fat:	1 g.
Cholesterol:	72 mg.
Sodium:	246 mg.
Fiber:	3 g.
Exchanges:	½ starch, 3 lean meat, 1 vegetable

Lemon Thyme Chicken with Vegetables

Baked Potatoes

Lime Chicken Fajitas ▶

½ teaspoon grated lime peel
2 tablespoons lime juice
1 tablespoon vegetable oil
2 cloves garlic, minced
½ teaspoon ground cumin
¼ teaspoon pepper

1 boneless whole chicken
   breast (8 to 10 oz.), skin
   removed, cut into 2 × ½-inch
   strips
1 cup julienne green pepper
   (2 × ¼-inch strips)
1 cup thinly sliced red onion
4 flour tortillas (8-inch)

4 servings

In 2-quart casserole, combine lime peel, lime juice, oil, garlic, cumin and pepper. Mix well. Add chicken. Toss to coat. Cover. Refrigerate 8 hours or overnight. Add green pepper and onion. Toss to coat. Re-cover. Microwave at High for 5 to 7 minutes, or until chicken is no longer pink, stirring twice. Set aside.

Place tortillas between 2 dampened paper towels. Microwave at High for 45 seconds to 1 minute, or until tortillas are warm to the touch.

Place one-fourth of chicken mixture on each tortilla. Fold up from bottom. Fold in sides and secure with wooden pick, leaving top open. Top with salsa and sour cream dairy blend, if desired.

Lime Chicken Fajitas

Corn, Cucumber & Avocado Salsa
(page 25)
Sour Cream Dairy Blend
Southwestern-style Cauliflower
(page 132)

Per Serving:			
Calories:	193	Cholesterol:	36 mg.
Protein:	16 g.	Sodium:	34 mg.
Carbohydrate:	20 g.	Fiber:	2 g.
Fat (total):	6 g.	Exchanges:	1 starch, 1½ lean meat, 1 vegetable
Saturated Fat:	1 g.		

Honey-Lemon Chicken

2 boneless whole chicken
   breasts (8 to 10 oz. each),
   split in half, skin removed
3 tablespoons honey, divided
2 teaspoons grated lemon
   peel, divided
3 tablespoons fresh lemon
   juice, divided
1 tablespoon low-sodium soy
   sauce
1 tablespoon cornstarch
½ teaspoon low-sodium instant
   chicken bouillon granules
½ cup water

4 servings

In 8-inch square baking dish, arrange chicken breast halves in even layer. In small bowl, combine 2 tablespoons honey, 1 teaspoon lemon peel, 1 tablespoon lemon juice and the soy sauce. Mix well. Pour over chicken breasts. Cover dish with wax paper. Microwave at High for 8 to 10 minutes, or until chicken is no longer pink and juices run clear, rearranging chicken 2 or 3 times. Set aside.

In 2-cup measure, combine cornstarch, the remaining 1 teaspoon lemon peel and the bouillon. Blend in water, the remaining 2 tablespoons lemon juice and 1 tablespoon honey. Microwave at High for 3 to 4 minutes, or until sauce is thickened and translucent, stirring every minute with whisk. Remove chicken from cooking liquid. Discard liquid. To serve, spoon 2 tablespoons sauce over each breast half.

Per Serving:			
Calories:	202	Cholesterol:	72 mg.
Protein:	27 g.	Sodium:	224 mg.
Carbohydrate:	16 g.	Fiber:	—
Fat (total):	3 g.	Exchanges:	3 lean meat, 1 fruit
Saturated Fat:	1 g.		

Honey-Lemon Chicken

Sesame Pasta & Vegetables (page 125)

Vegetarian Main Dishes

Plant proteins are identified as low-quality, or incomplete, protein because they lack some essential amino acids or do not contain them in correct amounts. When supplemented with a small amount of animal protein or combined with a complementary plant protein, they make excellent, nutritious, low-fat and high-fiber meals.

Use the photo chart to compensate for the deficiency in one plant protein by combining that protein with a complementary plant protein. Complementary proteins produce some classic combinations. Mix legumes with seeds — hummus (chickpeas and sesame paste) or grains: red beans and rice, peanut butter on bread, corn tortillas with refried beans. In addition to legume combinations, grains match well with milk products: macaroni and cheese, cereal with milk, rice pudding.

How to Match Up Complementary Proteins

Legumes

Milk

Grains

Breads, grains, rice

Legumes plus seeds = complete protein
Legumes plus breads or grains = complete protein
Breads, grains, rice plus
milk products (or legumes) = complete protein

Dried Beans, Peas & Lentils Equivalency Chart

Type	Amount	Yield	Serving Size
Green Split Peas, Great Northern Beans, Kidney Beans, Garbanzo Beans	1 lb.	6 cups	½ cup
Navy Beans	1 lb.	5 cups	½ cup
Lentils	1 lb.	5¾ cups	½ cup

How to Microwave Dried Beans, Peas & Lentils

Wash and sort beans or peas. In 3-quart casserole, combine beans with 6 cups hot water, 1 medium onion, chopped, and 1 bay leaf. Cover. Microwave at High for 10 minutes.

Microwave at 50% (Medium) for 1¼ to 2 hours longer, or until beans are tender, stirring twice. Add water, if needed, to keep beans just covered. Let stand, covered, for 10 minutes. Drain.

Lentils
Substitute 5-quart casserole for 3-quart casserole. Microwave at High for 10 minutes. Microwave at 50% (Medium) for 30 to 40 minutes longer. (Lentils not recommended for ovens with less than 600 cooking watts.)

Freeze cooked beans in 1-cup quantities, if desired. To defrost, unwrap and place beans in casserole. Cover. Microwave at High as directed in defrosting chart, right, stirring once. Let stand to complete defrosting.

Defrosting Beans, Peas & Lentils Chart

Amount	Casserole	Microwave at High
1 cup	1-quart	1½ to 2½ min.
2 cups	1-quart	2 to 4 min.
3 cups	2-quart	3 to 5 min.

Versatile Tofu

One of the most protein-rich and useful vegetable proteins is tofu, a bland, curdled soy milk available in two types. The custardy consistency of soft tofu makes it ideal for desserts, creamy dips, salad dressings and sauces. Slice, dice or crumble firm tofu for use as a meat alternative. To give firm tofu the texture of ground beef, drain and freeze; then defrost and crumble it.

Tofu is highly perishable and, depending on its freshness, will keep three to seven days in the refrigerator, but you must cover it with fresh water daily. If tofu sours, place it in fresh water and boil for three minutes; then drain and freeze it for use in casseroles.

How to Make Ground Tofu

Rinse and drain tofu. Seal in large plastic food-storage bag. Freeze at least 8 hours. Place frozen tofu in 1-quart casserole. Cover with wax paper.

Microwave at 30% (Medium Low) for 4 to 8 minutes, or until defrosted, stirring to break apart with fork and removing defrosted portions twice.

Place defrosted tofu in strainer. Drain, pressing to remove excess moisture. Crumble.

Black Bean Chili ▶

6 cups cooked black beans
  (page 102), divided
1¾ cups Low-fat Vegetable
  Broth (page 35)
½ cup chopped onion
½ cup thinly sliced celery
⅓ cup chopped green pepper
2 cloves garlic, minced
2 teaspoons olive oil
1 can (16 oz.) whole tomatoes,
  undrained and cut up
2 teaspoons chili powder
½ teaspoon ground cumin
½ teaspoon dried oregano
  leaves
¼ teaspoon salt
½ cup seeded chopped
  tomato
½ cup sliced green onions
2 tablespoons plus 2
  teaspoons sour cream
  dairy blend

6 to 8 servings

In food processor or blender, place 3 cups cooked beans and the broth. Process until smooth. Set aside.

In 3-quart casserole, combine onion, celery, pepper, garlic and oil. Cover. Microwave at High for 3 to 4 minutes, or until vegetables are tender-crisp, stirring once.

Add processed beans, the remaining 3 cups beans, the canned tomatoes, chili powder, cumin, oregano and salt. Mix well. Re-cover. Microwave at High for 12 to 18 minutes, or until chili is hot, stirring twice. Garnish each serving with 1 tablespoon each chopped tomato and onions, and 1 teaspoon sour cream dairy blend.

Per Serving:			
Calories:	244	Cholesterol:	2 mg.
Protein:	14 g.	Sodium:	205 mg.
Carbohydrate:	42 g.	Fiber:	14 g.
Fat (total):	3 g.	Exchanges:	2 starch, 2 vegetable, ½ fat
Saturated Fat:	1 g.		

Black Bean Chili

Cucumber Spears, Carrot Sticks, Pickled Peppers
Corn Bread

Lentil Stew

3 potatoes (about 6 oz. each),
  cut into 1-inch chunks
3 medium carrots, cut into
  2-inch chunks
2 ribs celery, cut into 2-inch
  chunks
1 medium onion, cut into 8
  wedges
½ cup water, divided
1 teaspoon dried marjoram
  leaves
¼ teaspoon salt
¼ teaspoon pepper
3 cups Low-fat Vegetable
  Broth (page 35)
1 can (16 oz.) whole tomatoes,
  undrained and cut up
1¼ cups uncooked lentils (8 oz.)
¼ cup all-purpose flour

8 servings

In 3-quart casserole, place potatoes, carrots, celery, onion, ¼ cup water, the marjoram, salt and pepper. Cover. Microwave at High for 10 to 12 minutes, or until vegetables are tender-crisp, stirring once. Add broth, tomatoes and lentils. Mix well.

In 1-cup measure, place remaining ¼ cup water and the flour. Blend with whisk. Add to stew. Mix well. Cover. Microwave at High for 10 minutes. Stir. Re-cover. Microwave at 50% (Medium) for 1 to 1¼ hours, or until lentils and vegetables are tender, stirring 3 times.

Per Serving:			
Calories:	190	Cholesterol:	—
Protein:	11 g.	Sodium:	230 mg.
Carbohydrate:	37 g.	Fiber:	9 g.
Fat (total):	1 g.	Exchanges:	2 starch, 1½ vegetable
Saturated Fat:	—		

Lentil Stew

Tossed Green Salad
Hearty Rye Bread Slices

Garbanzo Bean & Vegetable Pie

Nonstick vegetable cooking spray
2 cups seeded chopped tomatoes
1 yellow summer squash (about 6 oz.), cut in half lengthwise and thinly sliced (1½ cups)
1 zucchini (about 6 oz.), cut in half lengthwise and thinly sliced (1½ cups)
1 cup sliced fresh mushrooms
½ cup chopped onion
1 teaspoon dried basil leaves
½ teaspoon salt, divided
1 can (15 oz.) garbanzo beans, rinsed and drained
½ cup shredded hard farmer cheese (2 oz.), divided
1 cup uncooked couscous
1 cup Low-fat Vegetable Broth (page 35)
2 egg whites (¼ cup)
¼ cup snipped fresh parsley

8 servings

Spray 10-inch deep-dish pie plate with nonstick vegetable cooking spray. Set aside. In 3-quart casserole, combine tomatoes, squash, zucchini, mushrooms, onion, basil and ¼ teaspoon salt. Cover. Microwave at High for 6 to 9 minutes, or until vegetables are tender, stirring twice. Add beans and ¼ cup cheese. Mix well. Set aside.

In 4-cup measure, combine couscous, broth and remaining ¼ teaspoon salt. Cover with plastic wrap. Microwave at High for 2 to 2½ minutes, or until liquid is absorbed and couscous is tender. Let stand, covered, for 2 minutes.

Add egg whites and parsley to couscous. Mix well. Using back of spoon, press couscous mixture against bottom and up sides of prepared pie plate. Spoon vegetable mixture into couscous crust. Cover pie with plastic wrap. Microwave at High for 4 to 6 minutes, or until crust is firm and filling is hot, rotating pie plate once. Sprinkle top of pie with remaining ¼ cup cheese. Let stand until cheese is melted.

Per Serving:			
Calories:	181	Cholesterol:	7 mg.
Protein:	9 g.	Sodium:	203 mg.
Carbohydrate:	30 g.	Fiber:	5 g.
Fat (total):	3 g.	Exchanges:	1½ starch, ½ lean meat,
Saturated Fat:	1 g.		1 vegetable, ½ fat

Garbanzo Bean & Vegetable Pie

Fruit Salad of Grapes, Raspberries and Orange Segments

Spicy Bean & Rice Burrito Bake

¾ cup uncooked long-grain white rice

½ teaspoon dried oregano leaves

1½ cups Low-fat Chicken Broth (page 36) or defatted chicken broth

2 cups cooked Mexican Seasoned Pinto Beans (page 111)

1 can (8 oz.) whole tomatoes, drained and cut up

2 tablespoons sliced green onion

2 tablespoons canned chopped green chilies

¼ teaspoon salt

¼ teaspoon ground cumin

6 whole wheat flour tortillas (8-inch)

1 cup shredded hard farmer cheese (4 oz.)

½ cup seeded chopped tomato

6 servings

In 2-quart casserole, combine rice, oregano and broth. Cover. Microwave at High for 5 minutes. Microwave at 50% (Medium) for 12 to 16 minutes longer, or until rice is tender and liquid is absorbed. Set aside, covered. In 1-quart casserole, combine beans, canned tomatoes, the onion, chilies, salt and cumin. Mix well. Cover. Microwave at High for 4 to 6 minutes, or until mixture is hot, stirring once.

Spoon ⅓ cup bean mixture down center of each tortilla. Top each with ⅓ cup rice. Roll up, enclosing filling. Place seam-side-down in 10-inch square casserole. Sprinkle with cheese and chopped tomato. Microwave at High for 3 to 5 minutes, or until cheese is melted, rotating dish once. Serve with salsa.

Per Serving:			
Calories:	410	Cholesterol:	17 mg.
Protein:	17 g.	Sodium:	290 mg.
Carbohydrate:	69 g.	Fiber:	7 g.
Fat (total):	9 g.	Exchanges:	3 starch, 3 vegetable,
Saturated Fat:	4 g.		½ low-fat milk, 1 fat

Spicy Bean & Rice Burrito Bake

Corn, Cucumber & Avocado Salsa (page 25)
Salad of Greens, Jicama and Orange with
Sweet Apple & Poppy Seed Dressing (page 45)

Tamale Pie

Filling:

- 2 cups Mexican Seasoned Pinto Beans (page 110)
- 1 can (16 oz.) whole tomatoes, drained and cut up
- 1 pkg. (9 oz.) frozen corn
- 1 can (4 oz.) chopped green chilies
- ⅓ cup chopped green pepper
- ⅓ cup chopped onion
- ½ teaspoon ground cumin
- ¼ teaspoon dried cilantro leaves
- ¼ teaspoon dried oregano leaves
- ⅛ teaspoon garlic powder
- ½ cup yellow cornmeal
- ½ cup all-purpose flour
- 1 teaspoon baking powder
- ¼ teaspoon salt
- ½ cup skim milk
- 1 egg
- 1 tablespoon vegetable oil
- 1 teaspoon honey

6 servings

In 2-quart casserole, combine all filling ingredients. Mix well. Cover. Microwave at High for 10 to 12 minutes, or until filling is very hot and flavors are blended, stirring once or twice. Set aside, covered.

In small mixing bowl, combine cornmeal, flour, baking powder and salt. Add remaining ingredients. Mix just until blended. Spoon batter over top of bean mixture.

Microwave at High, uncovered, for 4 to 7 minutes, or until cornmeal topping is light and springy, not doughy, to the touch, rotating casserole 2 or 3 times. Let stand for 10 minutes. Sprinkle top with paprika, if desired.

Per Serving:	
Calories:	287
Protein:	13 g.
Carbohydrate:	52 g.
Fat (total):	4 g.
Saturated Fat:	1 g.
Cholesterol:	16 mg.
Sodium:	416 mg.
Fiber:	6 g.
Exchanges:	3 starch, 1½ vegetable, ½ fat

Tamale Pie

Green Onions, Carrot and Jicama Sticks

Spicy Pita Sandwich Spread ▶

- 2 cups cooked navy beans (page 102)
- 2 tablespoons water
- 2 teaspoons lime juice
- ⅛ teaspoon salt
- ⅓ cup finely chopped onion
- 1 teaspoon olive oil
- ¼ teaspoon paprika
- ¼ teaspoon ground cumin
- ¼ teaspoon dried oregano leaves
- 3 pitas (6-inch), cut in half crosswise
  Leaf lettuce
- 18 slices cucumber
- 2 Roma tomatoes, sliced (12 slices)

6 servings

In food processor or blender, place beans, water, lime juice and salt. Process until smooth. Set aside.

In 1-quart casserole, place onion, oil, paprika, cumin and oregano. Cover. Microwave at High for 2 to 3 minutes, or until onion is tender, stirring once.

Add bean mixture. Mix well. Re-cover. Microwave at High for 2 to 5 minutes, or until bean mixture is hot. Spread inside of each pita half with about ¼ cup bean mixture. Place lettuce inside each pita. Place 3 slices of cucumber and 2 slices of tomato inside each pita.

Per Serving:	
Calories:	168
Protein:	9 g.
Carbohydrate:	30 g.
Fat (total):	2 g.
Saturated Fat:	—
Cholesterol:	—
Sodium:	54 mg.
Fiber:	7 g.
Exchanges:	1½ starch, 1½ vegetable, ½ fat

California Bean Burgers

- ¼ cup low-fat or nonfat plain yogurt
- 2 teaspoons Dijon mustard
- 1¾ cups cooked red kidney beans (page 102) or 1 can (15 oz.) red kidney beans, rinsed and drained
- 2 tablespoons finely chopped carrot
- 2 tablespoons finely chopped green pepper
- 2 tablespoons finely chopped onion
- 1 teaspoon olive oil
- ½ teaspoon dried marjoram leaves
- ¼ cup plus 2 tablespoons unseasoned bread crumbs
- 1 egg
- 1 tablespoon sunflower nuts
  Nonstick vegetable cooking spray
- 4 whole wheat hamburger buns
  Lettuce
  Tomato

4 servings

In small bowl, combine yogurt and mustard. Mix well. Cover with plastic wrap and chill. In medium mixing bowl, mash beans with fork. Set aside.

In 1-quart casserole, combine carrot, green pepper, onion, oil and marjoram. Cover. Microwave at High for 3 to 4 minutes, or until vegetables are tender, stirring once. Add vegetables, bread crumbs, egg and sunflower nuts to beans. Mix well. Shape mixture into 4 patties, each a scant ½ cup.

Spray 10-inch nonstick skillet with nonstick vegetable cooking spray. Cook patties conventionally over medium-high heat, about 3 minutes on each side, until lightly browned. Serve in buns with lettuce, tomato and yogurt topping.

Per Serving:			
Calories:	294	Cholesterol:	71 mg.
Protein:	15 g.	Sodium:	386 mg.
Carbohydrate:	47 g.	Fiber:	4 g.
Fat (total):	6 g.	Exchanges:	3 starch, ½ vegetable, 1 fat
Saturated Fat:	1 g.		

Spicy Pita Sandwich Spread

Lemon Broccoli & Cauliflower Salad (page 46)

California Bean Burgers

Honey-Mustard Corn (page 130)

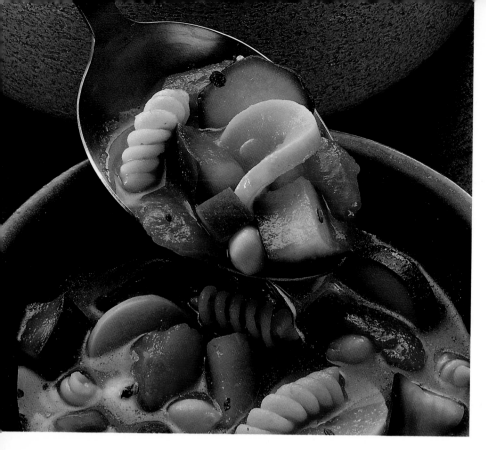

Eggplant Stew ▲

1 lb. eggplant, cubed (¾-inch cubes)
½ cup chopped onion
½ cup chopped green pepper
2 teaspoons olive oil
1 large clove garlic, minced
½ teaspoon dried oregano leaves
¼ teaspoon caraway seed
⅛ to ¼ teaspoon cayenne

1 can (28 oz.) whole tomatoes, undrained and cut up
1 can (15 oz.) garbanzo beans, rinsed and drained
1½ cups Low-fat Vegetable Broth (page 35)
½ cup uncooked rotini pasta
½ cup sliced yellow summer squash
½ cup sliced zucchini

8 servings

In 3-quart casserole, combine eggplant, onion, green pepper, oil, garlic and seasonings. Cover. Microwave at High for 12 to 15 minutes, or until eggplant is translucent and very tender, stirring 2 or 3 times.

Add remaining ingredients. Re-cover. Microwave at High for 23 to 26 minutes, or until flavors are blended and rotini is tender, stirring twice. Let stand, covered, for 10 minutes.

Per Serving:			
Calories:	135	Cholesterol:	—
Protein:	6 g.	Sodium:	192 mg.
Carbohydrate:	24 g.	Fiber:	6 g.
Fat (total):	2 g.	Exchanges:	1 starch, 2 vegetable, ½ fat
Saturated Fat:	—		

Eggplant Stew

Layered Lentil Loaf (page 22) with Crackers

Mexican Seasoned Pinto Beans

1 lb. dried pinto beans, washed and sorted
6 cups hot water
½ cup chopped onion
½ cup chopped green pepper
2 cloves garlic, minced
1 tablespoon chili powder
1 teaspoon ground cumin

10 servings, ½ cup each

In 3-quart casserole, combine all ingredients. Mix well. Cover. Microwave at High for 10 minutes. Microwave at 50% (Medium) for 1½ to 2 hours longer, or until beans are very tender, stirring twice and adding additional water, if necessary, to keep beans just covered.

Let stand, covered, for 10 minutes. Drain, if necessary. Freeze cooked beans in 1-cup quantities, if desired.

To defrost, microwave as directed in chart (page 102).

NOTE: This recipe is used in Spicy Bean & Rice Burrito Bake (page 107), Tamale Pie (page 108) and Mexican Pizza with Cornmeal Crust (opposite).

Per Serving:	
Calories:	333
Protein:	21 g.
Carbohydrate:	61 g.
Fat (total):	2 g.
Saturated Fat:	—
Cholesterol:	—
Sodium:	26 mg.
Fiber:	17 g.
Exchanges:	3½ starch, 2 vegetable

Mexican Pizza with Cornmeal Crust

Crust:

2⅓ cups hot water
1 cup yellow cornmeal
1 tablespoon margarine
¼ teaspoon salt
⅛ teaspoon cayenne

Toppings:

1 cup cooked Mexican
  Seasoned Pinto Beans (left)
¾ cup salsa
½ medium green pepper,
  thinly sliced
1 cup shredded hard farmer
  cheese (4 oz.)
1 cup shredded lettuce
½ cup seeded chopped
  tomato
2 tablespoons sliced green
  onion
3 large pitted black olives,
  sliced

8 servings

In 2-quart casserole, place water. Cover. Microwave at High for 6 to 8 minutes, or until water boils. Add remaining crust ingredients. Stir with whisk until smooth. Microwave, uncovered, at High for 2 to 3 minutes, or until mixture is very thick, stirring once or twice.

Spoon mixture onto 12-inch round platter. Spread in even layer with rubber scraper, mounding slightly around edges. Cover with plastic wrap. Set aside.

In 1-quart casserole, combine beans, salsa and green pepper. Mix well. Cover. Microwave at High for 3 to 4 minutes, or until pepper is tender-crisp, stirring once.

Spread mixture over crust. Sprinkle with cheese. Microwave at High for 1 to 2 minutes, or until cheese is melted, rotating platter once. Top with remaining ingredients. Serve in wedges with additional salsa, if desired.

Per Serving:			
Calories:	176	Cholesterol:	13 mg.
Protein:	8 g.	Sodium:	340 mg.
Carbohydrate:	22 g.	Fiber:	2 g.
Fat (total):	6 g.	Exchanges:	1 starch, ½ lean meat, 1 vegetable,
Saturated Fat:	3 g.		1 fat

Mexican Pizza with Cornmeal Crust

Salad of Fresh Greens and Orange Segments

Sweet & Sour Vegetables

1 cup diagonally sliced carrots
  (¼-inch slices)
1 cup green pepper chunks
  (¾-inch chunks)
¼ cup plus 2 tablespoons
  water, divided
½ cup Low-fat Vegetable or
  Chicken Broth (pages 35
  and 36)
¼ cup white vinegar
¼ cup packed brown sugar
2 tablespoons cornstarch
1 tablespoon vegetable oil
2 teaspoons low-sodium soy
  sauce
1 large clove garlic
2 cups cooked navy beans
  (page 102) or 1 can (16 oz.)
  navy beans, rinsed and
  drained
1 can (8 oz.) pineapple chunks
  in juice, drained
½ cup diagonally sliced green
  onions
3 cups hot cooked white rice

6 servings

In 2-quart casserole, place carrots, peppers and 2 tablespoons water. Cover. Microwave at High for 4½ to 6 minutes, or until vegetables are tender-crisp, stirring twice. Drain. Set aside.

In 4-cup measure, combine remaining ¼ cup water, the broth, vinegar, sugar, cornstarch, oil, soy sauce and garlic. Blend well with whisk. Microwave at High for 3½ to 4 minutes, or until sauce is thickened and translucent, stirring twice.

Add sauce and navy beans to vegetable mixture. Mix well. Cover. Microwave at High for 3 to 4 minutes, or until hot. Stir in pineapple and onions. Serve over rice.

Per Serving:			
Calories:	292	Cholesterol:	—
Protein:	8 g.	Sodium:	94 mg.
Carbohydrate:	59 g.	Fiber:	5 g.
Fat (total):	3 g.	Exchanges:	2 starch, 2½ vegetable,
Saturated Fat:	—		1 fruit, ½ fat

Sweet & Sour Vegetables

Spiced Shrimp Spring Rolls (page 28)

112

Fettucini Alfredo

⅔ cup low-fat dry milk powder
2 tablespoons all-purpose
   flour
1 clove garlic, minced
¼ teaspoon salt
¼ teaspoon pepper
¼ teaspoon ground nutmeg
1½ cups water
¼ cup shredded hard farmer
   cheese (1 oz.)
1 tablespoon grated
   Parmesan cheese
8 oz. uncooked fettucini
1 tablespoon snipped fresh
   parsley

4 servings

In 4-cup measure, combine dry milk, flour, garlic, salt, pepper and nutmeg. Blend in water. Microwave at High for 5 to 8 minutes, or until mixture thickens and bubbles, stirring with whisk every 2 minutes. Stir in cheeses. Cover with plastic wrap. Set aside.

Prepare fettucini as directed on package. Rinse and drain. Place in 2-quart casserole. Add sauce. Toss to coat. Cover. Microwave at High for 2 to 3 minutes, or until hot. Sprinkle with parsley.

Per Serving:	
Calories:	356
Protein:	19 g.
Carbohydrate:	57 g.
Fat (total):	5 g.
Saturated Fat:	3 g.
Cholesterol:	18 mg.
Sodium:	335 mg.
Fiber:	2 g.
Exchanges:	2½ starch, 1½ skim milk, 1 fat

Fettucini Alfredo

Tossed Green Salad
Toasted French Bread Slices

Four-cheese Stuffed Manicotti ▲

8 uncooked manicotti shells

Sauce:
1 can (16 oz.) whole tomatoes,
   undrained and cut up
1 can (8 oz.) tomato sauce
1 tablespoon Burgundy wine
2 teaspoons olive oil
½ teaspoon dried basil leaves

Filling:
1 carton (15 oz.) lite ricotta
   cheese (1 gm. fat per oz.)

½ cup low-fat cottage cheese,
   drained
2 egg whites (¼ cup)
2 tablespoons snipped fresh
   parsley
1 tablespoon grated Parmesan
   cheese
⅛ teaspoon garlic powder

½ cup shredded hard farmer
   cheese (2 oz.)

4 servings

Prepare manicotti shells as directed on package. Rinse. Let stand in warm water while preparing sauce and filling.

In 2-quart casserole, combine all sauce ingredients. Microwave at High, uncovered, for 6 to 8 minutes, or until flavors are blended and sauce is slightly thickened, stirring twice. Set aside.

In small mixing bowl, combine all filling ingredients. Stuff each cooked manicotti shell with scant ⅓ cup cheese filling.

Reserve ⅓ cup tomato sauce. Set aside. Pour remaining sauce into 10-inch square casserole. Arrange stuffed shells in sauce. Spoon reserved sauce over manicotti. Cover. Microwave at 70% (Medium High) for 12 to 14 minutes, or until hot, rotating dish twice. Sprinkle with farmer cheese. Let stand, covered, for 5 minutes, or until cheese is melted.

Per Serving:			
Calories:	367	Cholesterol:	32 mg.
Protein:	27 g.	Sodium:	836 mg.
Carbohydrate:	39 g.	Fiber:	3 g.
Fat (total):	12 g.	Exchanges:	2 starch, 2½ lean meat,
Saturated Fat:	6 g.		2 vegetable, ½ fat

Four-cheese Stuffed Manicotti

Toasted French Bread Slices with Fresh Garlic

Tofu Chili

8 oz. Ground Tofu (page 103)
½ cup chopped celery
½ cup chopped green pepper
½ cup chopped onion
2 teaspoons olive oil
1 large clove garlic, minced
1 can (16 oz.) kidney beans,
    rinsed and drained
1 can (16 oz.) whole tomatoes,
    undrained and cut up
1 can (16 oz.) tomato sauce
1½ teaspoons chili powder
¼ teaspoon ground cumin
    Dash cayenne

4 to 6 servings

In 3-quart casserole, place tofu, celery, pepper, onion, oil and garlic. Cover. Microwave at High for 6 to 8 minutes, or until vegetables are tender-crisp, stirring once. Add remaining ingredients. Microwave at High, uncovered, for 8 to 10 minutes, or until chili is hot and flavors are blended, stirring twice.

Per Serving:			
Calories:	149	Cholesterol:	—
Protein:	9 g.	Sodium:	601 mg.
Carbohydrate:	23 g.	Fiber:	7 g.
Fat (total):	4 g.	Exchanges:	1 starch, 1½ vegetable, 1 fat
Saturated Fat:	1 g.		

Tofu Chili

Seasoned Whole Wheat Tortilla Chips (page 25)
Toppings:
Shredded Hard Farmer Cheese (1 oz. per serving)
Chopped Green Pepper

◄ Lasagna Primavera

Nonstick vegetable cooking spray
9 uncooked lasagna noodles
2 cups fresh broccoli flowerets
2 cups sliced fresh mushrooms
1 yellow summer squash (about 4 oz.), sliced (1 cup)
1 zucchini (about 4 oz.), sliced (1 cup)
½ cup shredded carrot
1¼ cups water, divided
1 large clove garlic, minced
¼ teaspoon salt

¼ teaspoon pepper
½ cup nonfat dry milk powder
1 tablespoon plus 1 teaspoon all-purpose flour
½ teaspoon dried basil leaves
½ teaspoon fennel seed, crushed
½ teaspoon dried oregano leaves
1 cup lite ricotta cheese (1 gm. fat per oz.)
2 tablespoons snipped fresh parsley
1 cup shredded mozzarella cheese (4 oz.), divided

6 servings

Per Serving:	
Calories:	273
Protein:	19 g.
Carbohydrate:	37 g.
Fat (total):	6 g.
Saturated Fat:	3 g.
Cholesterol:	18 mg.
Sodium:	280 mg.
Fiber:	3 g.
Exchanges:	2 starch,
	1½ lean meat,
	1½ vegetable

Lasagna Primavera ·

Water Bagel Sticks

How to Microwave Lasagna Primavera

Spray 11 × 7-inch baking dish with nonstick vegetable cooking spray. Set aside. Prepare lasagna noodles as directed on package. Rinse. Let stand in warm water.

Combine broccoli, mushrooms, squash, zucchini, carrot, ¼ cup water, the garlic, salt and pepper in 3-quart casserole. Cover. Microwave at High for 8 to 10 minutes, or until vegetables are tender, stirring once. Set aside.

Place dry milk, flour, basil, fennel and oregano in 4-cup measure. Blend in remaining 1 cup water. Microwave at High for 3 to 5 minutes, or until mixture thickens and bubbles, stirring with whisk every minute. Set aside.

Combine ricotta cheese and parsley in small mixing bowl. Mix well. Set aside. Place lasagna noodles on paper towels to drain.

Layer 3 noodles, half of vegetable mixture, half of ricotta mixture, ½ cup mozzarella cheese and half of sauce in prepared dish. Top with 3 noodles, remaining vegetable and ricotta mixtures. Top with remaining noodles, sauce and mozzarella cheese.

Cover with plastic wrap. Microwave at 70% (Medium High) for 10 to 12 minutes, or until lasagna is hot, rotating dish once. Let stand, covered, for 10 minutes.

Spinach Soufflé

Nonstick vegetable cooking spray
- 1 pkg. (10 oz.) frozen chopped spinach
- 3 tablespoons all-purpose flour
- ¼ teaspoon dried dill weed
- ¼ teaspoon salt
- ¼ teaspoon pepper
- 1 cup skim milk
- 1 cup shredded hard farmer cheese (4 oz.)
- 2 egg yolks
- 5 egg whites (½ cup plus 2 tablespoons)

4 servings

Per Serving:	
Calories:	215
Protein:	17 g.
Carbohydrate:	12 g.
Fat (total):	11 g.
Saturated Fat:	6 g.
Cholesterol:	163 mg.
Sodium:	413 mg.
Fiber:	2 g.
Exchanges:	1½ lean meat, 1 vegetable, ½ skim milk, 1½ fat

Spinach Soufflé

Brandied Carrots (page 126)

How to Make Spinach Soufflé

Heat conventional oven to 350°F. Spray 1½-quart soufflé dish with nonstick vegetable cooking spray. Set aside. Unwrap spinach and place on plate. Microwave at High for 4 to 6 minutes, or until spinach is defrosted. Drain, pressing to remove excess moisture.

Place spinach in medium mixing bowl. Set aside. In 4-cup measure, combine flour, dill, salt and pepper. Blend in milk. Microwave at High for 2½ to 4 minutes, or until mixture thickens and bubbles, stirring every minute. Stir in cheese until melted.

Place egg yolks in small mixing bowl. Beat slightly. Stir small amount of hot mixture gradually into egg yolks. Blend egg yolks back into hot mixture. Add sauce to spinach. Mix well. Set aside.

Place egg whites in large mixing bowl. Beat at high speed of electric mixer until stiff but not dry. Fold into spinach mixture. Pour into prepared dish. Bake for 35 to 45 minutes, or until golden brown and knife inserted in center comes out clean. Serve immediately.

Creamy Pesto Vegetable Toss ▶

4 oz. uncooked linguine
1 tablespoon olive oil
1 tablespoon grated Parmesan
   cheese
1 tablespoon chopped walnuts
1 to 2 cloves garlic
1 cup packed fresh basil leaves
1 cup low-fat cottage cheese
2 medium yellow summer
   squash (6 oz. each), cut into
   2 × ¼-inch strips
2 medium zucchini (6 oz. each),
   cut into 2 × ¼-inch strips
2 large carrots, cut into 2 × ¼-
   inch strips
2 tablespoons water

4 servings

Prepare linguine as directed on package. Rinse and drain. Cover to keep warm. Set aside.

In food processor or blender, place oil, cheese, walnuts and garlic. Process until smooth. Gradually add basil and cottage cheese. Process until smooth. Set aside.

In 3-quart casserole, combine squash, zucchini, carrots and water. Cover. Microwave at High for 10 to 14 minutes, or until vegetables are tender, stirring once. Drain. Add cooked linguine and the basil mixture to vegetables. Toss to coat.

Per Serving:	
Calories:	255
Protein:	15 g.
Carbohydrate:	35 g.
Fat (total):	7 g.
Saturated Fat:	2 g.
Cholesterol:	6 mg.
Sodium:	281 mg.
Fiber:	5 g.
Exchanges:	1½ starch, 1 lean meat, 2½ vege-table, ½ fat

Creamy Pesto Vegetable Toss

Tossed Green Salad with Low-fat Oil & Vinegar Dressing (page 45)
Sesame Bread Sticks

Spaghetti Squash Primavera

1 large spaghetti squash
   (about 4 lbs.)
2 tablespoons lemon juice
1 tablespoon olive oil
1 clove garlic, minced
¼ teaspoon salt
2 cups fresh broccoli flowerets
8 oz. fresh mushrooms,
   quartered
2 tablespoons water

Sauce:
⅔ cup nonfat dry milk powder
2 tablespoons all-purpose
   flour
¼ teaspoon pepper
1½ cups water
½ cup shredded hard farmer
   cheese (2 oz.)
½ cup seeded chopped
   tomato

4 servings

Pierce squash rind deeply several times to allow steam to escape. Place squash on paper towel in microwave oven. Microwave at High for 20 to 25 minutes, or until rind softens, turning over once. Let stand 10 minutes.

In small bowl, combine lemon juice, oil, garlic and salt. Set aside. In 2-quart casserole, combine broccoli, mushrooms and water. Cover. Microwave at High for 4 to 6 minutes, or until vegetables are tender-crisp. Drain. Set aside.

In 4-cup measure, combine dry milk, flour and pepper. Blend in water. Microwave at High for 6 to 8 minutes, or until mixture thickens and bubbles, stirring every 2 minutes. Add cheese. Stir to melt cheese. Pour sauce over vegetables. Add tomato. Toss to coat. Cover to keep warm.

Cut squash in half crosswise. Scoop out and discard seeds and fibers. Twist away long strands of flesh with fork. Place in large mixing bowl. Add lemon juice mixture. Toss to coat. Serve squash topped with vegetables and sauce.

Per Serving:			
Calories:	307	Cholesterol:	17 mg.
Protein:	16 g.	Sodium:	377 mg.
Carbohydrate:	43 g.	Fiber:	8 g.
Fat (total):	9 g.	Exchanges:	2 starch, ½ lean meat,
Saturated Fat:	4 g.		2½ vegetable, 1½ fat

Spaghetti Squash Primavera

Crab & Cheese-stuffed Phyllo Bundles (page 29)

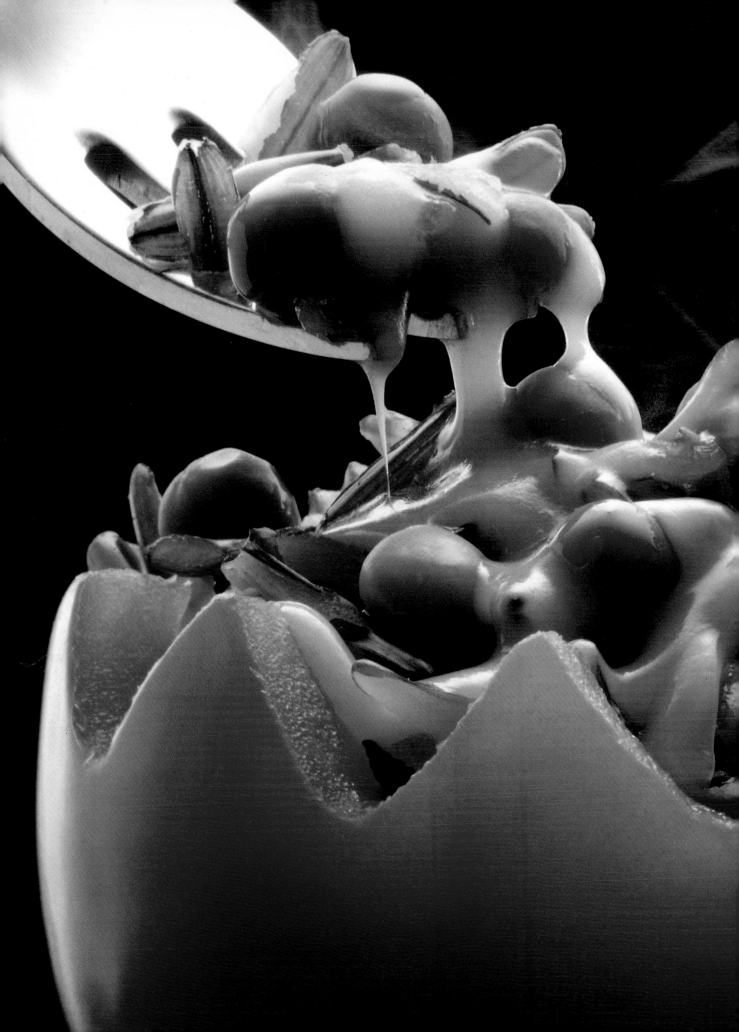

Vegetables

Three to five servings of vegetables, plus two to four servings of fruit each day should provide all the vitamins and minerals you need. Low-calorie, vitamin-rich vegetables also contribute fiber to your diet. Be sure to include some dark green or yellow vegetables in the daily menu. Overcooking and too much water leach the nutrients from vegetables. Conserve food value and flavor by microwaving them until just tender, but still crisp, in a minimum of water. To reduce fat and sodium, season vegetables with fresh lemon juice or a no-sodium seasoning mixture, opposite, instead of butter or margarine and salt. If you grow or buy fresh herbs and want to preserve them, you can dry them in the microwave oven, opposite.

Italian Herb Shaker

1 tablespoon plus 1 teaspoon dried basil leaves
2 teaspoons dried oregano leaves
1 teaspoon dried rosemary leaves
½ teaspoon crushed red pepper flakes

6 servings, 1 tsp. each

In small bowl, combine all ingredients. Mix well. Store in covered container in cool, dark place. Slightly crush mixture before using. Sprinkle on meats and poultry, and use for seasoning Italian sauces and pizza.

Indian Seasoning Medley

1 tablespoon fennel seed, crushed
2 teaspoons dried thyme leaves
1 teaspoon ground turmeric
¼ teaspoon cayenne

6 servings, 1 tsp. each

In small bowl, combine all ingredients. Mix well. Store in covered container in cool, dark place. Slightly crush mixture before using. Sprinkle seasoning on poultry, seafood and vegetables.

Southwest Seasoning

1 tablespoon plus 1 teaspoon dried parsley flakes
2 teaspoons dried cilantro leaves
1 teaspoon ground cumin
½ teaspoon garlic powder
½ teaspoon onion powder

6 servings, 1 tsp. each

In small bowl, combine all ingredients. Mix well. Store in covered container in cool, dark place. Slightly crush mixture before using. Sprinkle seasoning on poultry, seafood and vegetables.

Nutritional information not listed because amounts are negligible.

How to Microwave-dry Fresh Herbs

Wash and dry 1 bunch of fresh herbs. Strip leaves from stems; tear larger leaves in ½ to ¾-inch pieces. Loosely pack enough leaves to equal ½ cup. Place paper towel on plate. Sprinkle herbs evenly over towel.

Place ½ cup water in 1-cup measure; set next to plate in microwave oven. Microwave at High for 3¼ to 4 minutes, or just until leaves begin to feel dry and papery, tossing with fingers after first minute, and then every 45 seconds.

Watch closely to avoid over-drying. Sprinkle herbs evenly onto another paper towel. Let air-dry for 24 hours. When completely dry, store in airtight container in cool, dark place. Slightly crush dried herbs before measuring for use in recipes.

◄ Green & Wax Beans with Red Pepper Purée

- 1 large red pepper (8 oz.), seeded and cut into 1-inch chunks
- 1 teaspoon olive oil
- 1 clove garlic, minced
- ½ teaspoon red wine vinegar
- ¼ teaspoon low-sodium chicken bouillon granules
- ¼ teaspoon dried oregano leaves
- ½ lb. fresh green beans, trimmed
- ½ lb. fresh wax beans, trimmed
- ¼ cup water

6 servings

In 1-quart casserole, combine pepper, oil, garlic, vinegar, bouillon and oregano. Cover. Microwave at High for 8 to 11 minutes, or until pepper is very tender, stirring twice. In food processor or blender, process pepper mixture until smooth. Set aside.

In 2-quart casserole, place green beans, wax beans and water. Cover. Microwave at High for 12 to 14 minutes, or until tender, stirring twice. Drain. Arrange beans on serving platter. Spoon red pepper sauce over beans.

Per Serving:	
Calories:	38
Protein:	2 g.
Carbohydrate:	7 g.
Fat (total):	1 g.
Saturated Fat:	—
Cholesterol:	—
Sodium:	6 mg.
Fiber:	1 g.
Exchanges:	1½ vegetable

Brandied Carrots

- 2 cups julienne carrots (2 × ¼-inch strips)
- ¼ cup water
- 1 tablespoon brandy
- ½ teaspoon margarine
- ⅛ teaspoon salt

4 servings

In 1-quart casserole, place carrots and water. Cover. Microwave at High for 6 to 7 minutes, or until carrots are tender. Drain. Add brandy, margarine and salt. Toss to coat. Microwave at High for 1 to 1½ minutes, or until margarine is melted and flavors are blended, stirring once.

Per Serving:			
Calories:	40	Cholesterol:	—
Protein:	1 g.	Sodium:	94 mg.
Carbohydrate:	6 g.	Fiber:	2 g.
Fat (total):	1 g.	Exchanges:	1 vegetable, ½ fat
Saturated Fat:	—		

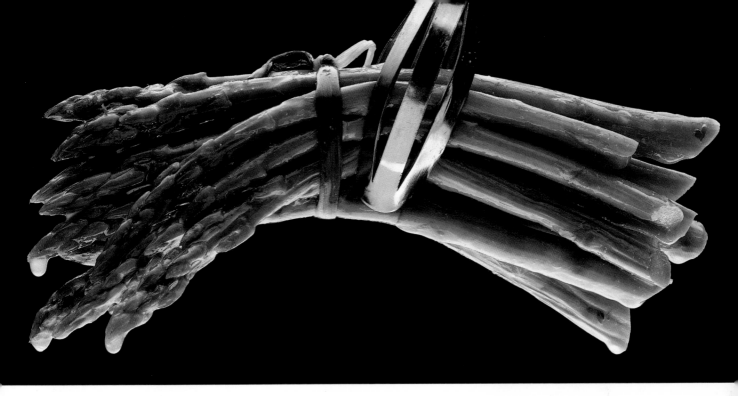

Asparagus Bundles

1 lb. fresh asparagus spears, cut into 7-inch lengths
2 tablespoons white wine vinegar
1 tablespoon olive oil
1 teaspoon snipped fresh parsley
¼ teaspoon dry mustard
¼ teaspoon sugar
1 green onion

4 servings

Per Serving:			
Calories:	35	Cholesterol:	—
Protein:	4 g.	Sodium:	2 mg.
Carbohydrate:	5 g.	Fiber:	2 g.
Fat (total):	1 g.	Exchanges:	1 vegetable
Saturated Fat:	—		

How to Microwave Asparagus Bundles

Arrange asparagus spears in even layer in 10-inch square casserole.

Combine vinegar, oil, parsley, dry mustard and sugar in 1-cup measure. Mix well. Pour over asparagus. Cover with plastic wrap. Microwave at High for 8 to 10 minutes, or until tender-crisp, rearranging spears from outside to center of dish once. Refrigerate, covered, overnight.

Cut away and discard white portion of green onion, leaving about 7 inches of green tops. Cut tops in half lengthwise, to yield 4 strips. Place in 9-inch pie plate. Cover with plastic wrap. Microwave at High for 30 to 45 seconds, or until strips are slightly limp.

Drain asparagus spears. Discard vinaigrette. Divide asparagus spears into 4 bunches. Place 1 onion ribbon around each bundle. Gently tie to secure bundles.

Sweet-spiced Brussels Sprouts & Apples

2 teaspoons packed brown sugar

⅛ teaspoon ground nutmeg

1 lb. fresh Brussels sprouts, trimmed and cut in half

¼ cup water

1 medium Rome apple, cored and cut into ½-inch cubes

1 teaspoon margarine

4 servings

In small bowl, combine brown sugar and nutmeg. Mix well. Set aside.

In 2-quart casserole, combine Brussels sprouts and water. Cover. Microwave at High for 6 to 8 minutes, or until tender-crisp. Drain. Add apples, margarine and brown sugar mixture. Mix well. Re-cover. Microwave at High for 1½ to 3 minutes, or until Brussels sprouts are tender and apples are soft, stirring once.

Per Serving:			
Calories:	82	Cholesterol:	—
Protein:	4 g.	Sodium:	37 mg.
Carbohydrate:	17 g.	Fiber:	5 g.
Fat (total):	1 g.	Exchanges:	2 vegetable, ½ fruit
Saturated Fat:	—		

Apple-glazed Peas, Carrots & Onions ▶

1 pkg. (10 oz.) frozen peas and carrots
1 cup frozen small whole onions
2 tablespoons water
3 tablespoons apple juice concentrate, undiluted
⅛ teaspoon ground cinnamon
Dash ground nutmeg

4 servings

In 2-quart casserole, combine peas and carrots, onions and water. Cover. Microwave at High for 7 to 10 minutes, or until vegetables are hot, stirring once. Drain. Add apple juice concentrate, cinnamon and nutmeg. Toss to coat. Microwave at High for 45 seconds to 1 minute, or until hot.

Per Serving:	
Calories:	71
Protein:	3 g.
Carbohydrate:	16 g.
Fat (total):	—
Saturated Fat:	—
Cholesterol:	—
Sodium:	55 mg.
Fiber:	4 g.
Exchanges:	1 starch

Wild Rice Stuffed Tomatoes

3 medium tomatoes (8 oz. each)
2 cups water
½ cup uncooked wild rice
½ cup frozen peas
¼ cup shredded hard farmer cheese
¼ teaspoon dried tarragon leaves

6 servings

Cut tomatoes in half crosswise. Scoop out pulp and seeds, leaving ¼-inch shells. Place tomatoes cut-sides-up in 10-inch square casserole. Set aside.

In 2-quart saucepan, place water and wild rice. Bring to boil conventionally over high heat. Reduce heat to low. Cover. Simmer for 45 to 50 minutes, or until rice kernels are open and almost all water is absorbed. Drain excess liquid. Stir in peas, cheese and tarragon.

Spoon ⅓ cup wild rice mixture into each tomato shell. Cover. Microwave at High for 4 to 8 minutes, or until tomatoes are tender and rice is hot, rotating dish once.

Per Serving:				
Calories:	79	Cholesterol:	4 mg.	
Protein:	4 g.	Sodium:	38 mg.	
Carbohydrate:	13 g.	Fiber:	1 g.	
Fat (total):	2 g.	Exchanges:	½ starch, 1 vegetable, ½ fat	
Saturated Fat:	1 g.			

Honey-Mustard Corn

  2 teaspoons margarine
1½ teaspoons honey
 ½ teaspoon stone-ground
      mustard
  4 fresh ears corn on the cob in
      husk (10 to 12 oz. each)

                     4 servings

In small bowl, microwave margarine at High for 15 to 30 seconds, or until melted. Add honey and mustard. Mix well. Set aside.

Gently pull back, but do not detach, husks. Remove silk. With pastry brush, brush each ear of corn with one-fourth of honey-mustard mixture. Pull husks up around corn. Gather ends of husks at top of ears and secure with string. Arrange ears on oven floor, at least 1½ inches apart. Microwave at High for 14 to 20 minutes, or until corn is tender, rotating and rearranging ears twice.

Per Serving:	
Calories:	91
Protein:	3 g.
Carbohydrate:	17 g.
Fat (total):	3 g.
Saturated Fat:	—
Cholesterol:	—
Sodium:	41 mg.
Fiber:	1 g.
Exchanges:	1 starch, ½ fat

Broccoli with Mustard-Cheese Sauce ▲

1 lb. fresh broccoli
¾ cup water, divided
¼ cup nonfat dry milk
2½ teaspoons all-purpose flour
Dash white pepper
⅓ cup shredded hard farmer
cheese (1 oz.)
½ teaspoon Dijon mustard

4 servings

Cut broccoli into spears. Trim and discard tough ends. In 10-inch square casserole, arrange broccoli spears with flowers toward center. Add ¼ cup water. Cover. Microwave at High for 8 to 12 minutes, or until tender, rotating dish once. Drain. Set aside.

In 4-cup measure, combine dry milk, flour and pepper. Blend in remaining ½ cup water. Mix well with whisk. Microwave at High for 2 to 2½ minutes, or until mixture thickens and bubbles, stirring twice. Stir in cheese and mustard. Pour over broccoli.

Per Serving:			
Calories:	84	Cholesterol:	8 mg.
Protein:	7 g.	Sodium:	113 mg.
Carbohydrate:	10 g.	Fiber:	3 g.
Fat (total):	2 g.	Exchanges:	½ lean meat, 2 vegetable
Saturated Fat:	1 g.		

Mushroom, Celery & Tomato Sauté

1 lb. whole fresh mushrooms
1 cup celery chunks (1-inch diagonal chunks)
2 tablespoons white-wine Worcestershire sauce
1 teaspoon margarine
¼ teaspoon salt
⅛ teaspoon garlic powder
½ cup quartered cherry tomatoes

6 servings

In 2-quart casserole, combine all ingredients, except cherry tomatoes. Cover. Microwave at High for 7 to 11 minutes, or until vegetables are tender, stirring twice. Add tomatoes. Toss to coat. Serve with slotted spoon.

Per Serving:			
Calories:	33	Cholesterol:	—
Protein:	2 g.	Sodium:	173 mg.
Carbohydrate:	5 g.	Fiber:	1 g.
Fat (total):	1 g.	Exchanges:	1 vegetable
Saturated Fat:	—		

Sweet & Sour Beets

2 cans (16 oz. each) small
  whole beets, rinsed and
  drained
1 small onion, thinly sliced
¼ cup cider vinegar

2 teaspoons sugar
1 teaspoon cornstarch
2 medium oranges, peeled and
  sectioned

6 servings

In 2-quart casserole, place beets and onion. Cover. Microwave at High for 8 to 10 minutes, or until onion is tender and beets are hot, stirring once. Set aside.

In 1-cup measure, combine vinegar, sugar and cornstarch. Blend with whisk. Microwave at High for 1 to 1½ minutes, or until mixture is thickened and translucent, stirring once or twice. Add vinegar mixture and orange sections to beets. Toss to coat.

Per Serving:			
Calories:	62	Cholesterol:	—
Protein:	1 g.	Sodium:	269 mg.
Carbohydrate:	15 g.	Fiber:	3 g.
Fat (total):	—	Exchanges:	1 vegetable, ½ fruit
Saturated Fat:			

Southwestern-style ▲ Cauliflower

4 cups fresh cauliflowerets
⅓ cup chopped red pepper
⅓ cup chopped yellow pepper
2 tablespoons canned
  chopped green chilies
1 teaspoon margarine
⅛ teaspoon ground cumin
¼ teaspoon salt

4 to 6 servings

In 2-quart casserole, combine all ingredients, except salt. Mix well. Cover. Microwave at High for 8 to 10 minutes, or until cauliflower is tender, stirring twice. Add salt. Mix well.

Per Serving:	
Calories:	27
Protein:	2 g.
Carbohydrate:	4 g.
Fat (total):	1 g.
Saturated Fat:	—
Cholesterol:	—
Sodium:	140 mg.
Fiber:	2 g.
Exchanges:	1 vegetable

Eggplant
& Pepper Kabobs

1 medium eggplant (about 1 lb.), cut into 6 slices and quartered
1 medium green pepper, cut into 16 chunks (about 1½-inch chunks)
1 medium red pepper, cut into 16 chunks (about 1½-inch chunks)
1 medium onion, cut into 8 wedges
2 tablespoons lemon juice
2 tablespoons olive oil
2 tablespoons water
1 teaspoon dried oregano leaves
1 teaspoon sugar
¼ teaspoon salt
⅛ teaspoon pepper
8 wooden skewers, 8-inch

8 servings

In large mixing bowl, place eggplant, peppers and onion. Set aside.

In 1-cup measure, combine all remaining ingredients. Blend with whisk. Microwave mixture at High for 45 seconds to 1 minute, or until hot. Pour over vegetables. Toss to coat. Cover with plastic wrap. Chill at least 2 hours, stirring once or twice.

On each skewer, thread 1 eggplant chunk, 1 chunk each of red and green pepper, 1 eggplant chunk, 1 onion wedge, 1 chunk each of red and green pepper. Finish with 1 eggplant chunk. Arrange kabobs in 10-inch square casserole. Cover. Microwave at High for 13 to 15 minutes, or until vegetables are tender, rotating dish twice. Serve hot or cold.

Per Serving:	
Calories:	57
Protein:	1 g.
Carbohydrate:	6 g.
Fat (total):	4 g.
Saturated Fat:	—
Cholesterol:	—
Sodium:	70 mg.
Fiber:	1 g.
Exchanges:	1 vegetable, ½ fat

Brown Rice with Toasted Pine Nuts

3 cups plus 2 tablespoons
    water, divided
1 cup uncooked long-grain
    brown rice
1 clove garlic, minced
1 teaspoon low-sodium chicken
    bouillon granules
½ teaspoon salt
⅛ teaspoon pepper
¼ cup pine nuts (1 oz.)
¾ cup finely chopped carrots
¼ cup snipped fresh parsley
2 tablespoons sliced green
    onion

6 servings

In 3-quart saucepan, combine 3 cups water, the rice, garlic, bouillon, salt and pepper. Bring to boil conventionally over high heat. Cover with tight-fitting lid. Reduce heat to low and simmer for 50 minutes, or until liquid is absorbed and rice is tender. Do not remove cover during cooking. While rice is simmering, heat conventional oven to 400°F.

In 8-inch square baking pan, bake pine nuts for 4 to 5 minutes, or until light golden brown, stirring twice. Set aside.

In 1-quart casserole, combine carrots and remaining 2 tablespoons water. Cover. Microwave at High for 3 to 4 minutes, or until carrots are tender-crisp. Drain. In medium mixing bowl, combine cooked rice, toasted pine nuts, the carrots, parsley and onion. Mix well.

Per Serving:			
Calories:	146	Cholesterol:	—
Protein:	4 g.	Sodium:	191 mg.
Carbohydrate:	27 g.	Fiber:	2 g.
Fat (total):	3 g.	Exchanges:	1 starch, 2 vegetable, ½ fat
Saturated Fat:	—		

Rosemary New Potatoes & Beans ▶

1 lb. new potatoes, sliced
    (¼-inch slices)
¼ cup julienne green pepper
    (1½ × ¼-inch strips)
¼ cup julienne red pepper
    (1½ × ¼-inch strips)
¼ cup chopped onion
2 tablespoons snipped fresh
    parsley
2 tablespoons Low-fat Chicken
    Broth (page 36) or defatted
    chicken broth
1 tablespoon olive oil
1 large clove garlic, minced
¼ teaspoon dried rosemary
    leaves, crushed
1 can (16 oz.) Great Northern
    beans or kidney beans,
    rinsed and drained

8 servings

In 2-quart casserole, combine all
ingredients, except beans. Cover.
Microwave at High for 10 to 14 minutes, or until potatoes are tender,
stirring once. Add beans. Mix well.
Microwave at High for 1½ to 2 minutes, or until beans are hot.

Per Serving:	
Calories:	107
Protein:	4 g.
Carbohydrate:	19 g.
Fat (total):	2 g.
Saturated Fat:	—
Cholesterol:	—
Sodium:	4 mg.
Fiber:	3 g.
Exchanges:	1 starch, 1 vegetable

Garlic Mashed Potatoes

4 medium potatoes (6 oz.
    each), peeled and cut into
    ½-inch cubes
¼ cup water
2 large cloves garlic, quartered

½ teaspoon salt
⅓ cup skim milk
1 tablespoon freeze-dried
    chives
    Paprika

4 to 6 servings

In 2-quart casserole, combine potatoes, water, garlic and salt. Cover.
Microwave at High for 10 to 14 minutes, or until potatoes are very tender, stirring twice. Add milk and chives. Beat at medium speed of
electric mixer until smooth. If necessary, microwave at High for 1 to 2
minutes, or until hot. Before serving, sprinkle with paprika.

Per Serving:			
Calories:	94	Cholesterol:	—
Protein:	2 g.	Sodium:	193 mg.
Carbohydrate:	21 g.	Fiber:	2 g.
Fat (total):	—	Exchanges:	1½ starch
Saturated Fat:	—		

◄ Rice & Vegetable Croquettes

¾ cup uncooked long-grain white rice
1½ cups plus 2 teaspoons water, divided
⅓ cup finely chopped red pepper
¼ cup shredded carrot
¼ cup sliced green onions
¼ teaspoon dried thyme leaves
1 egg white (2 tablespoons)
1 tablespoon all-purpose flour
¼ teaspoon salt
Nonstick vegetable cooking spray

4 servings

In 2-quart casserole, combine rice and 1½ cups water. Cover. Microwave at High for 5 minutes. Stir. Re-cover. Microwave at 50% (Medium) for 12 to 16 minutes, or until rice is tender and liquid is absorbed, stirring every 4 minutes. Set aside.

In 1-quart casserole, combine pepper, carrot, onions, the remaining 2 teaspoons water and the thyme. Cover. Microwave at High for 3 to 4 minutes, or until vegetables are tender, stirring once. Stir egg white, flour and salt into vegetable mixture. Add mixture to cooked rice. Mix well.

Measure ½ cup of rice mixture. Shape into 3½-inch patty. Repeat with remaining rice mixture. Spray 10-inch skillet with nonstick vegetable cooking spray. Heat skillet conventionally over medium heat. Place rice patties in skillet. Cook over medium-high heat for 4 to 7 minutes, or until light golden brown, turning patties once.

Per Serving:	
Calories:	147
Protein:	4 g.
Carbohydrate:	31 g.
Fat (total):	—
Saturated Fat:	—
Cholesterol:	—
Sodium:	151 mg.
Fiber:	1 g.
Exchanges:	1½ starch, 1 vegetable

Southern-style Succotash

1 can (16 oz.) black-eyed peas, rinsed and drained
1 can (8¾ oz.) corn, rinsed and drained
1 medium tomato, seeded and chopped
1 small zucchini, cubed (¼-inch cubes)
1 teaspoon margarine
½ teaspoon dried basil leaves
¼ teaspoon salt

6 servings

In 2-quart casserole, combine all ingredients. Mix well. Cover. Microwave at High for 7 to 10 minutes, or until succotash is hot and flavors are blended, stirring once or twice.

Per Serving:			
Calories:	81	Cholesterol:	—
Protein:	4 g.	Sodium:	180 mg.
Carbohydrate:	15 g.	Fiber:	5 g.
Fat (total):	1 g.	Exchanges:	1 starch
Saturated Fat:	—		

Herb & Orange Black Beans & Rice

1 cup uncooked long-grain
    white rice
1 bay leaf
½ teaspoon grated orange peel
½ teaspoon salt
¼ teaspoon dried thyme leaves
2 cups hot water
1 can (15 oz.) black beans,
    rinsed and drained
¼ cup chopped green pepper
¼ cup chopped onion

8 servings

In 2-quart casserole, combine rice, bay leaf, orange peel, salt and thyme. Add water. Cover. Microwave at High for 5 minutes. Microwave at 50% (Medium) for 15 to 21 minutes longer, or until rice is tender and liquid is absorbed. Let stand for 5 minutes. Remove and discard bay leaf.

Add beans. Mix well. Re-cover. Microwave at High for 1 to 2 minutes, or until hot. Sprinkle each serving with green pepper and onion.

Per Serving:			
Calories:	129	Cholesterol:	—
Protein:	5 g.	Sodium:	137 mg.
Carbohydrate:	27 g.	Fiber:	4 g.
Fat (total):	—	Exchanges:	1½ starch, ½ vegetable
Saturated Fat:	—		

Tri-bean Bake ▶

1   medium onion, thinly sliced
½   cup thinly sliced celery
1   tablespoon water
1   can (15 oz.) butter beans,
     rinsed and drained
1   can (15 oz.) garbanzo beans,
     rinsed and drained
1   can (15 oz.) pinto beans,
     rinsed and drained
1   can (8 oz.) tomato sauce
¼   cup apple juice concentrate,
     undiluted
1   teaspoon light molasses
¼   teaspoon dry mustard

10 servings

In 2-quart casserole, place onion, celery and water. Cover. Microwave at High for 3 to 6 minutes, or until vegetables are tender, stirring once. Add remaining ingredients. Mix well. Re-cover. Microwave at High for 13 to 15 minutes, or until mixture is hot and flavors are blended, stirring twice.

Per Serving:	
Calories:	131
Protein:	7 g.
Carbohydrate:	25 g.
Fat (total):	1 g.
Saturated Fat:	—
Cholesterol:	—
Sodium:	157 mg.
Fiber:	7 g.
Exchanges:	1 starch, 2 vegetable

Molded Vegetable & Saffron Pasta ▲

4   oz. uncooked Acini di Pepe
     macaroni (scant ¾ cup)
1   pkg. (10 oz.) frozen chopped
     broccoli
2   tablespoons finely chopped
     onion
⅛   teaspoon ground saffron

1   tablespoon sliced pimiento
½   teaspoon grated lemon peel
½   teaspoon salt
1   egg white (2 tablespoons)
     Nonstick vegetable cooking
     spray

6 servings

Prepare macaroni as directed on package. Rinse and drain. Cover. Set aside. In 2-quart casserole, place broccoli, onion and saffron. Cover. Microwave at High for 4 to 6 minutes, or until broccoli is hot and onion is tender-crisp, stirring once. Add pimiento, lemon peel, salt, cooked macaroni and the egg white. Mix well.

Spray each of six 6-ounce custard cups with nonstick vegetable cooking spray. Place heaping ½ cup of macaroni mixture in each cup. Microwave at High for 3 to 6 minutes, or until hot, rearranging cups once. To serve, invert cups onto dinner plates.

Per Serving:		Cholesterol:	—
Calories:	87	Sodium:	200 mg.
Protein:	4 g.	Fiber:	2 g.
Carbohydrate:	17 g.	Exchanges:	½ starch, 2 vegetable
Fat (total):	—		
Saturated Fat:	—		

Curried Rice with Pears & Raisins

2 cups hot water
1 cup uncooked long-grain white rice
1 medium pear, cored and cut into ½-inch cubes (about 1 cup)
¼ cup raisins
1 teaspoon curry powder
½ teaspoon salt

6 servings

In 2-quart casserole, combine all ingredients. Cover. Microwave at High for 5 minutes. Microwave at 50% (Medium) for 20 to 25 minutes longer, or until rice is tender and liquid is absorbed. Let stand, covered, for 5 minutes. Before serving, fluff with fork.

Per Serving:			
Calories:	157	Cholesterol:	—
Protein:	3 g.	Sodium:	183 mg.
Carbohydrate:	36 g.	Fiber:	1 g.
Fat (total):	—	Exchanges:	1½ starch, 1 fruit
Saturated Fat:	—		

Desserts

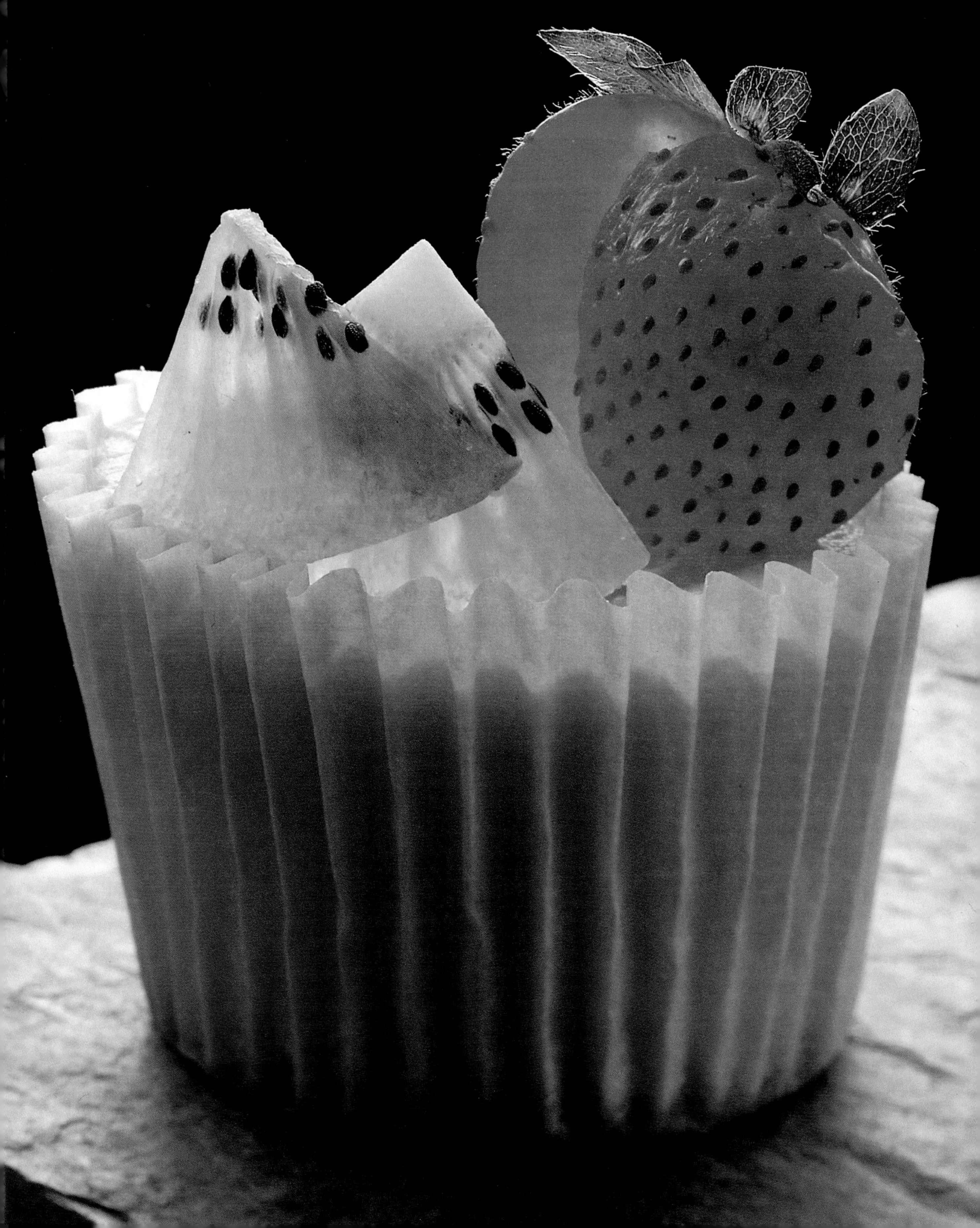

Fruit Desserts

A dessert of refreshing fruit satisfies part of the two to four servings per day requirement. Nothing beats homegrown fruits during their brief season. At other times, modern shipping technology brings us fresh fruits from worldwide sources.

For a dinner party, or to turn a family meal into a special occasion, experiment with the more exotic fruits. This photo chart of a selection of less-familiar fruits shows each serving next to a whole, ripe specimen so you can identify them.

Red bananas

Ugli Fruit

Cherimoya (Custard Apple)

Feijoa (Pineapple Guava)

Kadota Fig

Kiwano

Kiwifruit

Mango

Tamarillos

Many fruits must be shipped while still firm and may need ripening at home, generally at room temperature, uncovered and out of direct sunlight. Your produce manager will help you recognize ripe fruits. If you buy smooth passion fruits, allow them to become wrinkled and shriveled before serving them. Some fruits, like Asian pears, bananas, cherimoyas and feijoas darken when exposed to light. Coat cut surfaces with fresh lemon or lime juice.

Blood Orange

Papaya

Passion Fruit

Golden Raspberries

Kumquats

Asian Pears

Crenshaw Melon

Yellow Watermelon

Santa Claus Melon

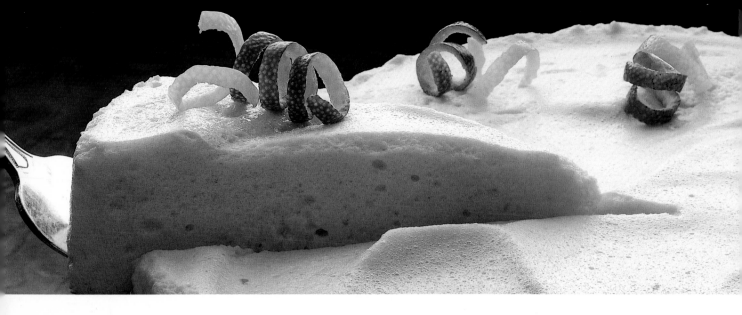

Lemon-Lime Seafoam Pie

⅓ cup graham cracker crumbs
1 pkg. (3 oz.) lime gelatin
1 cup hot water
1 teaspoon grated lemon peel

2 tablespoons fresh lemon juice
1 can (12 oz.) evaporated skim
  milk, chilled

10 servings

Per Serving:	
Calories:	71
Protein:	4 g.
Carbohydrate:	14 g.
Fat (total):	—
Saturated Fat:	—
Cholesterol:	1 mg.
Sodium:	87 mg.
Fiber:	—
Exchanges:	½ fruit, ½ skim milk

How to Microwave Lemon-Lime Seafoam Pie

Sprinkle graham cracker crumbs evenly in bottom of 10-inch spring-form pan. Set aside. Place gelatin in medium mixing bowl. Set aside.

Place water in 2-cup measure. Cover with plastic wrap. Microwave at High for 1½ to 3 minutes, or until boiling. Add to gelatin. Stir until dissolved.

Add lemon peel and juice. Chill until soft set, about 45 minutes to 1 hour, stirring twice. Remove from refrigerator. Set aside.

Place milk in large mixing bowl. Beat at high speed of electric mixer until thick and foamy, about 1 minute. Add gelatin mixture. Continue beating until combined.

Spoon mixture into prepared pan. Spread evenly. Chill 4 hours, or until firm. Run thin-bladed spatula around edges to loosen. Remove side of pan.

Place pie on serving platter. Garnish with lemon and lime slices or zest, if desired.

Strawberry-Raspberry Fondue ▶

1 pkg. (16 oz.) frozen
   unsweetened whole
   strawberries
½ cup low-sugar red raspberry
   spread

Dippers:
   Cantaloupe spears
   Whole fresh strawberries
   Fresh banana spears
   Pretzel twists or sticks
   Angel food cake, torn into
   bite-size pieces

   18 servings, 2 tbsp. each

In 2-quart casserole, combine
frozen strawberries and raspberry
spread. Cover. Microwave at High
for 6 to 8 minutes, or until strawberries are defrosted and hot, stirring twice. In food processor or
blender, process mixture until
smooth. Pour into serving dish.
Cover with plastic wrap. Chill 4
hours, or until cold. Serve with
desired dippers.

Per Serving:	
Calories:	34
Protein:	—
Carbohydrate:	9 g.
Fat (total):	—
Saturated Fat:	—
Cholesterol:	—
Sodium:	12 mg.
Fiber:	1 g.
Exchanges:	½ fruit

Peach Fondue ▲

1 pkg. (16 oz.) frozen
   unsweetened sliced
   peaches
½ cup low-sugar orange
   marmalade spread

Dippers:
   Cantaloupe spears
   Whole fresh strawberries
   Fresh banana spears
   Pretzel twists or sticks
   Angel food cake, torn into
   bite-size pieces

   18 servings, 2 tbsp. each

In 2-quart casserole, combine peaches and marmalade. Cover. Microwave at High for 8 to 10 minutes, or until peaches are defrosted and
hot, stirring twice. In food processor or blender, process mixture until
smooth. Pour into serving dish. Cover with plastic wrap. Chill 4 hours,
or until cold. Serve with desired dippers.

Per Serving:			
Calories:	34	Cholesterol:	—
Protein:	—	Sodium:	13 mg.
Carbohydrate:	9 g.	Fiber:	—
Fat (total):	—	Exchanges:	½ fruit
Saturated Fat:	—		

Tangerine Yogurt Ice

5 tangerines (about 7 oz. each)
1 cup hot water
½ cup sugar
½ cup vanilla-flavored low-fat
yogurt

6 servings, ½ cup each

Cut peel and white membrane from tangerines with sharp knife. Hold fruit over bowl to catch juice. Cut to center between fruit segments and dividing membranes, releasing fruit into bowl.

In food processor or blender, process sectioned fruit and any reserved juice until smooth (2 cups puréed fruit). Set aside.

In 4-cup measure, combine water and sugar. Microwave at High for 2 to 4 minutes, or until very hot and sugar is dissolved, stirring once or twice. Add puréed fruit to sugar-water mixture. Stir to combine.

Pour into 9-inch round cake dish. Freeze for 4 to 6 hours, or until firm, stirring once every hour to break apart. Cover with plastic wrap and freeze overnight, if desired.

If frozen overnight, let stand at room temperature for 10 minutes. Place tangerine ice in food processor or blender. Add yogurt. Process until smooth. Return to dish. Freeze until serving time. To serve, scoop mixture into balls.

Grapefruit Yogurt Ice: Follow recipe as directed, except substitute 2 grapefruit (1¼ lbs. each) for tangerines.

Per Serving:	
Calories:	105
Protein:	1 g.
Carbohydrate:	25 g.
Fat (total):	—
Saturated Fat:	—
Cholesterol:	1 mg.
Sodium:	15 mg.
Fiber:	2 g.
Exchanges:	1½ fruit

Tropical Papaya Yogurt Ice ▲

2 papayas (16 oz. each),
   peeled, cut in half lengthwise
   and seeded
1 tablespoon fresh lime juice

1 cup hot water
½ cup sugar
½ cup vanilla-flavored low-fat
   yogurt

6 servings, ½ cup each

Cut papayas into chunks. Place fruit and lime juice in food processor or blender. Process until smooth (2 cups puréed fruit). Set aside.

In 4-cup measure, combine water and sugar. Microwave at High for 2 to 4 minutes, or until very hot and sugar is dissolved, stirring once or twice. Add puréed fruit to sugar-water mixture. Stir to combine.

Pour into 9-inch round cake dish. Freeze for 4 to 6 hours, or until firm, stirring once every hour to break apart. Cover with plastic wrap and freeze overnight, if desired.

If frozen overnight, let stand at room temperature for 10 minutes. Place papaya ice in food processor or blender. Add yogurt. Process until smooth. Return to dish. Freeze until serving time. To serve, scoop mixture into balls.

Per Serving:			
Calories:	114	Cholesterol:	1 mg.
Protein:	2 g.	Sodium:	16 mg.
Carbohydrate:	28 g.	Fiber:	1 g.
Fat (total):	—	Exchanges:	2 fruit
Saturated Fat:	—		

Strawberry Tofu Pie

1 lb. fresh strawberries, hulled
¾ cup hot water
1 pkg. (0.3 oz.) sugar-free
   strawberry gelatin
3 oz. light cream cheese
   (Neufchâtel)
1 lb. soft tofu, rinsed and
   drained (about 2½ cups)

8 servings

Reserve 5 whole strawberries for garnish. Slice remaining strawberries in ¼-inch slices. Arrange about 21 slices around sides of 9-inch pie plate. Set remaining strawberry slices aside.

In 2-cup measure, place water. Cover with plastic wrap. Microwave at High for 1½ to 3 minutes, or until boiling. Add gelatin. Stir until gelatin dissolves. Set aside.

In small mixing bowl, microwave cheese at High for 15 to 30 seconds, or until softened. In food processor or blender, place reserved strawberry slices, the cheese, gelatin mixture and tofu. Process until smooth. Pour into pie plate. Cover with plastic wrap. Refrigerate at least 8 hours, or until set. Slice reserved strawberries for garnish.

Per Serving:			
Calories:	90	Cholesterol:	8 mg.
Protein:	6 g.	Sodium:	96 mg.
Carbohydrate:	7 g.	Fiber:	2 g.
Fat (total):	5 g.	Exchanges:	1 lean meat, ½ fruit
Saturated Fat:	2 g.		

Mini Fruit-topped Cheesecakes

6 vanilla wafer cookies
   (1½-inch)
2 oz. light cream cheese
   (Neufchâtel)
1 cup lite ricotta cheese (1 gm.
   fat per oz.)
1 egg
¼ cup sugar
2 tablespoons all-purpose flour
1 tablespoon grated lemon
   peel
1 teaspoon fresh lemon juice
1 teaspoon vanilla

Strawberry slices
Kiwifruit slices
Fresh pineapple wedges

6 servings

Line each of 6 microwave muffin cups with 2 paper liners. Place 1 cookie in bottom of each cup. Set aside.

In medium mixing bowl, micro-wave cream cheese at High for 15 to 30 seconds, or until soft-ened. Add ricotta cheese. Beat at medium speed of electric mixer until mixture is smooth. Add re-maining ingredients, except top-ping. Beat at medium speed of electric mixer until combined. Spoon evenly into prepared liners.

Microwave at High for 4 to 6 min-utes, or until cheesecakes are set in center, rotating dish every 2 min-utes. Let cool for 10 minutes in muffin pan. Remove cheesecakes from pan and place on cooling rack. Remove outer liners. Cool for 30 minutes. Chill at least 2 hours. Decorate top of each cheesecake with strawberries, kiwifruit and pineapple.

Per Serving:	
Calories:	154
Protein:	7 g.
Carbohydrate:	20 g.
Fat (total):	5 g.
Saturated Fat:	3 g.
Cholesterol:	60 mg.
Sodium:	90 mg.
Fiber:	2 g.
Exchanges:	½ lean meat, 1 fruit, ½ skim milk, ½ fat

Blackberry Pavlovas

- 1 cup powdered sugar
- 2 tablespoons cornstarch
- 4 egg whites (½ cup), room temperature
- ¼ teaspoon cream of tartar
- ¼ teaspoon vanilla
- 1 pkg. (0.8 oz.) sugar-free vanilla pudding and pie filling
- 1½ cups skim milk
- 1 can (16½ oz.) blackberries, drained

6 servings

Per Serving:	
Calories:	144
Protein:	5 g.
Carbohydrate:	31 g.
Fat (total):	—
Saturated Fat:	—
Cholesterol:	1 mg.
Sodium:	86 mg.
Fiber:	3 g.
Exchanges:	1½ fruit, ½ skim milk

How to Make Blackberry Pavlovas

Heat conventional oven to 250°F. Line baking sheet with parchment paper. Trace six 3½-inch circles on paper. Set aside. Sift powdered sugar and cornstarch together. Set aside.

Place egg whites, cream of tartar and vanilla in large mixing bowl. Beat at high speed of electric mixer until soft peaks begin to form.

Add powdered sugar mixture, 1 tablespoon at a time, while beating at high speed. Beat until mixture is stiff and glossy.

Spread about ½ cup meringue mixture over each circle on prepared baking sheet, mounding slightly around edges. Bake for 2 hours. Turn oven off. Do not open door. Let meringues stand in oven for 1 hour. Remove from oven and cool to room temperature. Set aside.

Combine pudding mix and milk in 4-cup measure. Stir with whisk to combine. Microwave at High for 4 to 6 minutes, or until mixture thickens slightly and comes to a boil, stirring with whisk every 2 minutes. Place plastic wrap directly on surface of pudding. Chill until cold, about 4 hours.

Peel paper carefully from meringues. Place meringues on serving platter. Spoon about ¼ cup pudding into each meringue. Top evenly with blackberries.

149

Mocha Mousse

¼ cup water
1 envelope (0.25 oz.) unflavored gelatin
1 carton (8 oz.) coffee-flavored low-fat yogurt
4 egg whites (½ cup), room temperature
3 tablespoons sugar
1 teaspoon vanilla

6 servings

In 1-cup measure, place water. Sprinkle unflavored gelatin over water. Let stand for 5 minutes. Microwave at High for 30 seconds to 1¼ minutes, or until gelatin is dissolved, stirring once. Set aside. In small mixing bowl, place yogurt. Add gelatin mixture. Mix well. Set aside.

In medium mixing bowl, beat egg whites at high speed of electric mixer until foamy. Gradually add sugar, 1 tablespoon at a time, while continuing to beat at high speed. Beat until stiff, but not dry, peaks form. Fold gelatin mixture and vanilla into beaten egg whites. Spoon mousse evenly into eight 6-ounce custard cups or individual dessert dishes. Chill 2 hours, or until set. Before serving, sprinkle lightly with cocoa, if desired.

Per Serving:			
Calories:	71	Cholesterol:	2 mg.
Protein:	5 g.	Sodium:	60 mg.
Carbohydrate:	12 g.	Fiber:	—
Fat (total):	—	Exchanges:	½ fruit, ½ skim milk
Saturated Fat:	—		

◄ Pear Phyllo Tart

Nonstick vegetable cooking spray
2 tablespoons packed brown sugar
2 teaspoons cornstarch
¼ teaspoon ground cinnamon
¼ teaspoon ground nutmeg
½ cup water

2 medium pears, cored, cut in half lengthwise and sliced (¼-inch slices)
2 tablespoons raisins
⅓ cup butter or margarine
10 sheets frozen phyllo (17 × 12-inch sheets), thawed

10 servings

Per Serving:	
Calories:	114
Protein:	1 g.
Carbohydrate:	14 g.
Fat (total):	7 g.
Saturated Fat:	4 g.
Cholesterol:	17 mg.
Sodium:	119 mg.
Fiber:	1 g.
Exchanges:	1 fruit, 1 fat

Heat conventional oven to 375°F. Spray 12-inch pizza pan with non-stick vegetable cooking spray. Set aside. Continue with photo directions, below.

How to Make Pear Phyllo Tart

Combine sugar, cornstarch, cinnamon and nutmeg in 2-quart casserole. Blend in water. Add pear slices and raisins. Mix well. Cover.

Microwave at High for 6 to 8 minutes, or until pears are tender and mixture is thickened and translucent, stirring 3 times. Set aside.

Place butter in small bowl. Microwave at High for 1¼ to 1½ minutes, or until melted. Set aside.

Unroll and remove phyllo sheets. Cover with plastic wrap. Working quickly, brush each sheet lightly with butter. Fold lengthwise into thirds. Cover with plastic wrap.

Arrange phyllo strips in spoke-like fashion on prepared pan; overlap ends in center. Brush with remaining butter. Loosely twist each strip, and coil to form roll just inside edge of pan.

Spread pear mixture in center of pastry. Bake for 20 to 25 minutes, or until golden brown. Serve in wedges, warm or cold.

Chocolate-Banana Cheesecake

Crust:
- 2 teaspoons margarine
- ½ cup old-fashioned rolled oats
- 2 tablespoons packed brown sugar

Filling:
- 4 oz. light cream cheese (Neufchâtel)
- 1 egg
- 1 egg white (2 tablespoons)
- ½ cup lite ricotta cheese (1 gm. fat per oz.)

- ½ cup evaporated skim milk
- ½ cup sugar
- ⅓ cup cocoa
- 1 medium banana, mashed
- 2 tablespoons all-purpose flour
- 1 teaspoon vanilla

Topping:
- ¼ cup vanilla-flavored low-fat yogurt
- 2 tablespoons sour cream dairy blend

10 servings

Per Serving:			
Calories:	164	Cholesterol:	39 mg.
Protein:	6 g.	Sodium:	118 mg.
Carbohydrate:	24 g.	Fiber:	2 g.
Fat (total):	6 g.	Exchanges:	½ fruit, 1 skim milk, 1 fat
Saturated Fat:	3 g.		

How to Microwave Chocolate-Banana Cheesecake

Place margarine in 9-inch round cake dish. Microwave at High for 30 to 45 seconds, or until melted. Stir in oats and brown sugar. Mix well.

Press mixture firmly against bottom of dish. Microwave at High for 1½ to 3 minutes, or until set, rotating dish once. Set aside.

Place cheese in 8-cup measure or 2-quart casserole. Microwave cheese at High for 30 to 45 seconds, or until softened. Add remaining filling ingredients. Beat at medium speed of electric mixer until well blended.

Microwave mixture at High for 3 to 4 minutes, or until mixture is very hot and starts to set, beating with whisk every minute. Pour filling over prepared crust.

Place dish on saucer in microwave oven. Microwave at 50% (Medium) for 4 to 8 minutes, or until center is almost set, rotating dish twice (filling becomes firm as it cools). Chill 1 hour.

Combine topping ingredients in small mixing bowl. Stir until smooth. Spread topping evenly over cheesecake. Cover with plastic wrap. Refrigerate at least 8 hours or overnight. Garnish with banana slices, if desired.

Orange-soaked Angel Cake

1 angel food cake (8 or 9-inch round), about 1½ lbs.
1 pint fresh strawberries, sliced
1 cup fresh blueberries
2 kiwifruit, peeled, cut in half lengthwise and sliced
¼ cup low-sugar apricot spread
½ cup water
¼ cup sugar
2 tablespoons Grand Marnier liqueur or orange juice

12 servings

Place cake on serving platter. Using meat fork, pierce top of cake at 1-inch intervals. Set aside. In large mixing bowl, combine fruits. Set aside.

In small mixing bowl, microwave apricot spread at High for 45 seconds to 1 minute, or until melted, stirring once. Over 2-cup measure, press spread through wire strainer, using back of spoon. Discard pulp. Add water, sugar and liqueur to apricot spread. Mix well.

Microwave at High for 1 to 2 minutes, or until sugar is dissolved, stirring once. Pour syrup over fruit. Toss to coat. Spoon fruit and syrup mixture over cake, allowing syrup to soak into cake. Cover cake with plastic wrap. Chill 4 hours before serving.

Per Serving:			
Calories:	201	Cholesterol:	—
Protein:	4 g.	Sodium:	93 mg.
Carbohydrate:	47 g.	Fiber:	2 g.
Fat (total):	—	Exchanges:	1½ starch, 1½ fruit
Saturated Fat:	—		

Index

A

Acorn Squash,
  Orange-gingered Acorn Squash, 124
Almonds,
  Peach & Chicken Almond Ding, 97
Angel Food Cake,
  Orange-soaked Angel Cake, 153
Appetizers & Snacks, 18-31
  Artichokes with Hungarian Dipping
    Sauce, 24
  Cheese & Basil Pepper Spirals, 30
  Cheese & Vegetable Nachos, 26
  Corn, Cucumber & Avocado Salsa, 25
  Crab & Cheese-stuffed Phyllo
    Bundles, 29
  Feta & Pepper Crisps, 31
  Garlic-Chive Potato Crisps, 31
  Hot Pepper Cheese Spread, 20
  Layered Lentil Loaf, 22
  Mosaic French Bread Pizza, 22
  Raspberry Fruit Dip, 20
  Seasoned Whole Wheat Tortilla
    Chips, 25
  Spiced Shrimp Spring Rolls, 28
  Tangy Vegetable Dip, 21
  Thai-style Skewered Chicken, 27
  Tropical Fruit & Cheese Log, 24
Apples,
  Apple-glazed Peas, Carrots
    & Onions, 129
  Curry Chicken & Apple Soup, 39
  Herb Turkey Patties with Apple
    Chutney, 89
  Sweet Apple & Poppy Seed
    Dressing, 45
  Sweet-spiced Brussels Sprouts
    & Apples, 128

Apricot-sauced Turkey Tenderloins, 86
Artichokes with Hungarian Dipping
  Sauce, 24
Asparagus,
  Asparagus Bundles, 127
  Curried Chicken with Asparagus
    & Raspberries, 92
Avocados,
  Corn, Cucumber & Avocado Salsa, 25

B

Bananas,
  Chocolate-Banana Cheesecake, 152
Barbecued Chicken Sandwich, 96
Basil,
  Cheese & Basil Pepper Spirals, 30
  Shrimp & Basil Pizza, 75
Beans,
  Black Bean Chili, 104
  California Bean Burgers, 109
  Defrosting Beans, Peas & Lentils
    Chart, 102
  Dried Beans, Peas & Lentils
    Equivalency Chart, 102
  Garbanzo Bean & Vegetable Pie, 106
  Green & Wax Beans with Red Pepper
    Purée, 126
  Herb & Orange Black Beans
    & Rice, 137
  Mexican Seasoned Pinto Beans, 110
  Rosemary New Potatoes & Beans, 135
  Spicy Bean & Rice Burrito Bake, 107
  Tri-bean Bake, 138
  Turkey Sausage & Bean Soup, 43
Beef,
  also see: Ground Beef
  Fats & Cholesterol Comparison, 59
  Italian Herbed Steak Strips, 62
  Zesty Mexican Rolled Steak, 64
Beets,
  Sweet & Sour Beets, 132
Bisque,
  Crab Bisque, 40
Black Beans,
  Black Bean Chili, 104
  Herb & Orange Black Beans
    & Rice, 137
Blackberry Pavlovas, 149
Bouquet Garni,
  How to Make Bouquet Garni, 35
Brandied Carrots, 126
Bread,
  Mosaic French Bread Pizza, 22
Broccoli,
  Broccoli with Mustard-Cheese
    Sauce, 131
  Lemon Broccoli & Cauliflower
    Salad, 46
Broiled Tuna Steaks with Kiwi-Papaya
  Salsa, 69
Broths,
  Broth Defrosting Chart, 37
  Low-fat Chicken Broth, 36
  Low-fat Vegetable Broth, 35
  Two Methods to Defat Broth, 37

Brown Rice & Shrimp Salad, 50
Brown Rice with Toasted Pine Nuts, 134
Brussels Sprouts,
  Sweet-spiced Brussels Sprouts
    & Apples, 128
Burgers,
  California Bean Burgers, 109
Burritos,
  Spicy Bean & Rice Burrito Bake, 107

C

Cajun Skewered Shrimp, 77
Cake,
  Orange-soaked Angel Cake, 153
California Bean Burgers, 109
Cardamom Orange Spinach Salad, 47
Carrots,
  Apple-glazed Peas, Carrots
    & Onions, 129
  Brandied Carrots, 126
  Spiced Chayote & Carrots, 125
Casseroles,
  Creamy Chicken & Vegetable
    Casserole, 95
  Garbanzo Bean & Vegetable Pie, 106
  Greek Lasagna Pie, 85
  Lamb & Spinach Pie, 64
  Lasagna Primavera, 115
  Spicy Bean & Rice Burrito Bake, 107
  Tamale Pie, 108
  Tri-bean Bake, 138
  Turkey Eggplant Bake, 88
Cauliflower,
  Lemon Broccoli & Cauliflower
    Salad, 46
  Southwestern-style Cauliflower, 132
Celery,
  Mushroom, Celery & Tomato Sauté, 131
Chayote,
  Spiced Chayote & Carrots, 125
Cheese,
  Broccoli with Mustard-Cheese
    Sauce, 131
  Cheese & Basil Pepper Spirals, 30
  Cheese & Vegetable Nachos, 26
  Crab & Cheese-stuffed Phyllo
    Bundles, 29
  Creamy Parmesan Dressing, 45
  Feta & Pepper Crisps, 31
  Feta & Spinach-stuffed Chicken
    Breasts, 93
  Four-cheese Stuffed Manicotti, 113
  Hot Pepper Cheese Spread, 20
  Jumbo Crab & Cheese-stuffed
    Mushrooms, 78
  Tropical Fruit & Cheese Log, 24
Cheesecakes,
  Chocolate-Banana Cheesecake, 152
  Mini Fruit-topped Cheesecakes, 148
Chicken,
  Barbecued Chicken Sandwich, 96
  Chicken & Shrimp Gumbo, 38
  Creamy Chicken & Vegetable
    Casserole, 95

Creole Chicken Breasts, 92
Curried Chicken with Asparagus
 & Raspberries, 92
Curry Chicken & Apple Soup, 39
Feta & Spinach-stuffed Chicken
 Breasts, 93
Grilled Chicken Salad, 53
Honey-Lemon Chicken, 99
How to Bone a Half Chicken Breast, 80
Hungarian Chicken Breasts, 94
Lemon Thyme Chicken with
 Vegetables, 98
Lime Chicken Fajitas, 99
Low-fat Chicken Broth, 36
Oriental Chicken Salad, 55
Peach & Chicken Almond Ding, 97
Thai-style Skewered Chicken, 27
Chili,
 Black Bean Chili, 104
 Tofu Chili, 114
Chips,
 Seasoned Whole Wheat Tortilla
  Chips, 25
Chives,
 Cold Poached Salmon with Lemon-
  Chive Sauce, 71
 Garlic-Chive Potato Crisps, 31
Chocolate-Banana Cheesecake, 152
Cholesterol,
 Fats & Cholesterol Comparison of
  Fish & Seafood, 67
 Fats & Cholesterol Comparison of
  Lean Meats, 59
 Fats & Cholesterol Comparison of
  Skinned Poultry, 80
Chops,
 Honey-Mustard Glazed Pork Chops, 60
Chunky Italian Meat Sauce, 62
Chutney,
 Herb Turkey Patties with Apple
  Chutney, 89
Cider-sauced Turkey Breast, 90
Clams,
 Linguine & Red Clam Sauce, 79
 Manhattan Clam Stew, 42
Cold Lemon Cucumber Soup, 40
Cold Poached Salmon with Lemon-
 Chive Sauce, 71
Corn,
 Corn, Cucumber & Avocado Salsa, 25
 Honey-Mustard Corn, 130
Cornmeal,
 Mexican Pizza with Cornmeal
  Crust, 111
Crab,
 Crab & Cheese-stuffed Phyllo
  Bundles, 29
 Crab Bisque, 40
 Crunchy Crab Salad in Tomato
  Cups, 49
 Jumbo Crab & Cheese-stuffed
  Mushrooms, 78
Cranberries,
 Frosted Cranberry Soup, 43
Creamy Chicken & Vegetable
 Casserole, 95
Creamy Italian Dressing, 45
Creamy Parmesan Dressing, 45

Creamy Pesto Vegetable Toss, 119
Creamy Potato & Wild Rice Soup, 39
Creole,
 Creole Chicken Breasts, 92
 Halibut with Creole Relish, 74
Croquettes,
 Rice & Vegetable Croquettes, 136
Crunchy Crab Salad in Tomato Cups, 49
Crustaceans,
 Fats & Cholesterol Comparison, 67
Cucumbers,
 Cold Lemon Cucumber Soup, 40
 Corn, Cucumber & Avocado Salsa, 25
Cumin Citrus Scallops, 79
Curried Chicken with Asparagus
 & Raspberries, 92
Curried Rice with Pears & Raisins, 139
Curry Chicken & Apple Soup, 39

D

Defrosting,
 Broth Defrosting Chart, 37
 Defrosting Beans, Peas & Lentils
  Chart, 102
Desserts, 141-153
 Blackberry Pavlovas, 149
 Chocolate-Banana Cheesecake, 152
 Fruit Desserts, 142
 Grapefruit Yogurt Ice, 146
 Lemon-Lime Seafoam Pie, 144
 Mini Fruit-topped Cheesecakes, 148
 Mocha Mousse, 150
 Orange-soaked Angel Cake, 153
 Peach Fondue, 145
 Pear Phyllo Tart, 151
 Strawberry Tofu Pie, 147
 Strawberry-Raspberry Fondue, 145
 Tangerine Yogurt Ice, 146
 Tropical Papaya Yogurt Ice, 146
Dietary Guidelines, 6
Dill,
 Lemon Dill Sole in Parchment, 72
Dips,
 Corn, Cucumber & Avocado Salsa, 25
 Raspberry Fruit Dip, 20
 Tangy Vegetable Dip, 21
Dressings,
 Creamy Italian Dressing, 45
 Creamy Parmesan Dressing, 45
 French Dressing, 45
 Low-fat Oil & Vinegar Dressing, 45
 Peppercorn Dressing, 45
 Sweet Apple & Poppy Seed
  Dressing, 45
 Tips to Reduce Fat in Salad
  Dressings, 45
Dried Beans, Peas & Lentils
 Equivalency Chart, 102

E

Eggplant,
 Eggplant & Pepper Kabobs, 133
 Eggplant Stew, 110
 Turkey Eggplant Bake, 88

F

Fajitas,
 Lime Chicken Fajitas, 99
Fats,
 Comparison of Fats & Oils, 12
 Fats & Cholesterol Comparison of
  Fish & Seafood, 67
 Fats & Cholesterol Comparison of
  Lean Meats, 59
 Fats & Cholesterol Comparison of
  Skinned Poultry, 80
 Hidden Fat, 14
 Tips for Reducing Fat in Salad
  Dressings, 45
 Tips for Reducing Fats, 14
 Two Methods to Defat Broth, 37
 Types of Fats, 11
Feta & Pepper Crisps, 31
Feta & Spinach-stuffed Chicken
 Breasts, 93
Fettucini Alfredo, 113
Fillets,
 Japanese Marinated Salmon Fillets, 70
 Mint-Raspberry Salmon Fillets, 70
Finfish,
 Fats & Cholesterol Comparison, 67
Fish, 68-74
 Broiled Tuna Steaks with Kiwi-Papaya
  Salsa, 69
 Cold Poached Salmon with Lemon-
  Chive Sauce, 71
 Fats & Cholesterol Comparison, 67
 Fresh Catch with Yogurt Tartar
  Sauce, 74
 Halibut with Creole Relish, 74
 Japanese Marinated Salmon Fillets, 70
 Lemon Dill Sole in Parchment, 72
 Mint-Raspberry Salmon Fillets, 70
 Orange Roughy with Kiwi-Orange
  Sauce, 69
 Red Snapper with Mustard Cream
  Sauce, 72
 Tropical Sweet & Sour Swordfish, 68
Fondues,
 Peach Fondue, 145
 Strawberry-Raspberry Fondue, 145
Four-cheese Stuffed Manicotti, 113
French Bread,
 Mosaic French Bread Pizza, 22
French Dressing, 45
Fresh Catch with Yogurt Tartar Sauce, 74
Frosted Cranberry Soup, 43
Fruits,
 also see: names of individual fruits
 Fruit Desserts, 142
 Mini Fruit-topped Cheesecakes, 148
 Raspberry Fruit Dip, 20
 Tropical Fruit & Cheese Log, 24

G

Garbanzo Bean & Vegetable Pie, 106
Garlic Mashed Potatoes, 135
Garlic-Chive Potato Crisps, 31

Grapefruit,
  Grapefruit Yogurt Ice, 146
  Honey-Raspberry Grapefruit Salad, 47
Greek Lasagna Pie, 85
Green Beans,
  Green & Wax Beans with Red Pepper
    Purée, 126
Grilled Chicken Salad, 53
Ground Beef,
  Chunky Italian Meat Sauce, 62
  Taco Salad, 65
Gumbo,
  Chicken & Shrimp Gumbo, 38

H

Halibut with Creole Relish, 74
Height & Weight Tables, 5
Herbs,
  Herb & Orange Black Beans
    & Rice, 137
  Herb Turkey Patties with Apple
    Chutney, 89
  How to Microwave-dry Fresh
    Herbs, 123
  Italian Herb Shaker, 123
Honey-Lemon Chicken, 99
Honey-Mustard Corn, 130
Honey-Mustard Glazed Pork Chops, 60
Honey-Raspberry Grapefruit Salad, 47
Hot Pepper Cheese Spread, 20
Hungarian Chicken Breasts, 94

I

Indian Seasoning Medley, 123
Italian Dressing,
  Creamy Italian Dressing, 45
Italian Herb Shaker, 123
Italian Herbed Steak Strips, 62

J

Jambalaya,
  Shrimp Jambalaya, 77
Japanese Marinated Salmon Fillets, 70
Jumbo Crab & Cheese-stuffed
  Mushrooms, 78

K

Kabobs,
  Cajun Skewered Shrimp, 77
  Eggplant & Pepper Kabobs, 133
  Pepper Steak Kabobs, 61
  Thai-style Skewered Chicken, 27
Kiwifruit,
  Broiled Tuna Steaks with Kiwi-Papaya
    Salsa, 69
  Orange Roughy with Kiwi-Orange
    Sauce, 69

L

Lamb,
  Fats & Cholesterol Comparison, 59
  Lamb & Spinach Pie, 64
Lasagna,
  Greek Lasagna Pie, 85
  Lasagna Primavera, 115
Layered Lentil Loaf, 22
Lean Meats, 59-65
  Fats & Cholesterol Comparison of
    Lean Meats, 59
Leeks,
  Saffron Squash & Leek Soup, 41
Lemons,
  Cold Lemon Cucumber Soup, 40
  Cold Poached Salmon with Lemon-
    Chive Sauce, 71
  Honey-Lemon Chicken, 99
  Lemon Broccoli & Cauliflower
    Salad, 46
  Lemon Dill Sole in Parchment, 72
  Lemon Thyme Chicken with
    Vegetables, 98
  Lemon-Lime Seafoam Pie, 144
Lentils,
  Defrosting Beans, Peas & Lentils
    Chart, 102
  Dried Beans, Peas & Lentils
    Equivalency Chart, 102
  Layered Lentil Loaf, 22
  Lentil Stew, 104
Lime,
  Lemon-Lime Seafoam Pie, 144
  Lime Chicken Fajitas, 99
Linguine & Red Clam Sauce, 79
Lo Mein,
  Tofu Lo Mein, 116
Low-fat Chicken Broth, 36
Low-fat Oil & Vinegar Dressing, 45
Low-fat Vegetable Broth, 35

M

Main Dishes, 56-119
Mandarin Oranges,
  Veal Scallops with Mandarin Orange
    Sauce, 63
Manhattan Clam Stew, 42
Manicotti,
  Four-cheese Stuffed Manicotti, 113
Marinated Pork Medallion Salad, 52
Marsala,
  Turkey Marsala, 87
Mashed Potatoes,
  Garlic Mashed Potatoes, 135
Meats, 59-65
  Chunky Italian Meat Sauce, 62
  Fats & Cholesterol Comparison of
    Lean Meats, 59
  Honey-Mustard Glazed Pork Chops, 60
  Italian Herbed Steak Strips, 62
  Lamb & Spinach Pie, 64
  Pepper Steak Kabobs, 61
  Pineapple-stuffed Pork Tenderloin, 60
  Sesame Pork, 61
  Taco Salad, 65

  Veal Scallops with Mandarin Orange
    Sauce, 63
  Zesty Mexican Rolled Steak, 64
Mexican Pizza with Cornmeal Crust, 111
Mexican Seasoned Pinto Beans, 110
Mini Fruit-topped Cheesecakes, 148
Mint-Raspberry Salmon Fillets, 70
Mocha Mousse, 150
Molded Vegetable & Saffron Pasta, 138
Mollusks,
  Fats & Cholesterol Comparison, 67
Mosaic French Bread Pizza, 22
Mousse,
  Mocha Mousse, 150
Mushrooms,
  Jumbo Crab & Cheese-stuffed
    Mushrooms, 78
  Mushroom, Celery & Tomato Sauté, 131
  Mushroom Stroganoff, 117
Mustard,
  Broccoli with Mustard-Cheese
    Sauce, 131
  Honey-Mustard Corn, 130
  Honey-Mustard Glazed Pork Chops, 60
  Red Snapper with Mustard Cream
    Sauce, 72

N

Nachos,
  Cheese & Vegetable Nachos, 26
New Potatoes,
  Rosemary New Potatoes & Beans, 135
Nutritional Information, 16
Nuts,
  Brown Rice with Toasted Pine Nuts, 134
  Peach & Chicken Almond Ding, 97

O

Oils,
  Comparison of Fats & Oils, 12
  Low-fat Oil & Vinegar Dressing, 45
Onions,
  Apple-glazed Peas, Carrots
    & Onions, 129
Orange Roughy with Kiwi-Orange
  Sauce, 69
Oranges,
  Cardamom Orange Spinach Salad, 47
  Herb & Orange Black Beans
    & Rice, 137
  Orange Roughy with Kiwi-Orange
    Sauce, 69
  Orange-gingered Acorn Squash, 124
  Orange-soaked Angel Cake, 153
  Veal Scallops with Mandarin Orange
    Sauce, 63
Oriental Chicken Salad, 55
Oriental Scallop & Pasta Salad, 48

P

Papayas,
  Broiled Tuna Steaks with Kiwi-Papaya
    Salsa, 69

Tropical Papaya Yogurt Ice, 146
Parmesan Cheese,
   Creamy Parmesan Dressing, 45
Pasta,
   Creamy Pesto Vegetable Toss, 119
   Fettucini Alfredo, 113
   Four-cheese Stuffed Manicotti, 113
   Linguine & Red Clam Sauce, 79
   Molded Vegetable & Saffron Pasta, 138
   Oriental Scallop & Pasta Salad, 48
   Sesame Pasta & Vegetables, 125
Patties,
   Herb Turkey Patties with Apple
      Chutney, 89
Peach & Chicken Almond Ding, 97
Peach Fondue, 145
Pears,
   Curried Rice with Pears & Raisins, 139
   Pear Phyllo Tart, 151
Peas,
   Apple-glazed Peas, Carrots
      & Onions, 129
   Defrosting Beans, Peas & Lentils
      Chart, 102
   Dried Beans, Peas & Lentils
      Equivalency Chart, 102
   Yellow Split Pea & Vegetable Soup, 41
Peppercorn Dressing, 45
Peppers,
   Cheese & Basil Pepper Spirals, 30
   Eggplant & Pepper Kabobs, 133
   Feta & Pepper Crisps, 31
   Green & Wax Beans with Red Pepper
      Purée, 126
   Hot Pepper Cheese Spread, 20
   Pepper Steak Kabobs, 61
Pesto,
   Creamy Pesto Vegetable Toss, 119
Phyllo,
   Crab & Cheese-stuffed Phyllo
      Bundles, 29
   Pear Phyllo Tart, 151
   Turkey Salad in Phyllo Bowls, 82
Pies,
   Garbanzo Bean & Vegetable Pie, 106
   Greek Lasagna Pie, 85
   Lamb & Spinach Pie, 64
   Lemon-Lime Seafoam Pie, 144
   Strawberry Tofu Pie, 147
   Tamale Pie, 108
Pine Nuts,
   Brown Rice with Toasted Pine Nuts, 134
Pineapple,
   Pineapple-stuffed Pork Tenderloin, 60
   Teriyaki Turkey with Pineapple Rice, 91
Pinto Beans,
   Mexican Seasoned Pinto Beans, 110
Pitas,
   Spicy Pita Sandwich Spread, 109
Pizzas,
   Feta & Pepper Crisps, 31
   Mexican Pizza with Cornmeal
      Crust, 111
   Mosaic French Bread Pizza, 22
   Shrimp & Basil Pizza, 75
Poppy Seed,
   Sweet Apple & Poppy Seed
      Dressing, 45

Pork,
   Fats & Cholesterol Comparison, 59
   Honey-Mustard Glazed Pork Chops, 60
   Marinated Pork Medallion Salad, 52
   Pineapple-stuffed Pork Tenderloin, 60
   Sesame Pork, 61
Potatoes,
   Creamy Potato & Wild Rice Soup, 39
   Garlic Mashed Potatoes, 135
   Garlic-Chive Potato Crisps, 31
   Rosemary New Potatoes & Beans, 135
Poultry, 80-99
   Apricot-sauced Turkey Tenderloins, 86
   Barbecued Chicken Sandwich, 96
   Chicken & Shrimp Gumbo, 38
   Cider-sauced Turkey Breast, 90
   Creamy Chicken & Vegetable
      Casserole, 95
   Creole Chicken Breasts, 92
   Curried Chicken with Asparagus
      & Raspberries, 92
   Curry Chicken & Apple Soup, 39
   Fats & Cholesterol Comparison of
      Skinned Poultry, 80
   Feta & Spinach-stuffed Chicken
      Breasts, 93
   Grilled Chicken Salad, 53
   Herb Turkey Patties with Apple
      Chutney, 89
   Honey-Lemon Chicken, 99
   How to Bone a Half Chicken Breast, 80
   Hungarian Chicken Breasts, 94
   Lemon Thyme Chicken with
      Vegetables, 98
   Lime Chicken Fajitas, 99
   Low-fat Chicken Broth, 36
   Oriental Chicken Salad, 55
   Peach & Chicken Almond Ding, 97
   Tandoori Turkey & Rice, 89
   Teriyaki Turkey with Pineapple Rice, 91
   Thai-style Skewered Chicken, 27
   Turkey Eggplant Bake, 88
   Turkey Sausage & Bean Soup, 43
   Turkey Marsala, 87
   Turkey Salad in Phyllo Bowls, 82
   Wheat Berry & Turkey Salad, 51
   Wild Rice-filled Turkey Roll, 86
Primavera,
   Lasagna Primavera, 115
   Spaghetti Squash Primavera, 119
Proteins,
   How to Match Up Complementary
      Proteins, 101

R

Raisins,
   Curried Rice with Pears & Raisins, 139
Raspberries,
   Curried Chicken with Asparagus
      & Raspberries, 92
   Honey-Raspberry Grapefruit Salad, 47
   Mint-Raspberry Salmon Fillets, 70
   Raspberry Fruit Dip, 20
   Strawberry-Raspberry Fondue, 145
Red Peppers,
   Green & Wax Beans with Red Pepper
      Purée, 126

Red Snapper with Mustard Cream
   Sauce, 72
Relishes,
   Halibut with Creole Relish, 74
Rice,
   Brown Rice & Shrimp Salad, 50
   Brown Rice with Toasted Pine Nuts, 134
   Creamy Potato & Wild Rice Soup, 39
   Curried Rice with Pears & Raisins, 139
   Herb & Orange Black Beans
      & Rice, 137
   Rice & Vegetable Croquettes, 136
   Spicy Bean & Rice Burrito Bake, 107
   Tandoori Turkey & Rice, 89
   Teriyaki Turkey with Pineapple Rice, 91
   Wild Rice Stuffed Tomatoes, 129
   Wild Rice-filled Turkey Roll, 86
Rosemary New Potatoes & Beans, 135

S

Saffron,
   Molded Vegetable & Saffron Pasta, 138
   Saffron Squash & Leek Soup, 41
Salad Dressings,
   see: Dressings
Salads, 44-55
   Brown Rice & Shrimp Salad, 50
   Cardamom Orange Spinach Salad, 47
   Crunchy Crab Salad in Tomato
      Cups, 49
   Grilled Chicken Salad, 53
   Honey-Raspberry Grapefruit Salad, 47
   How to Select, Store & Prepare Salad
      Greens, 44
   Lemon Broccoli & Cauliflower
      Salad, 46
   Marinated Pork Medallion Salad, 52
   Oriental Chicken Salad, 55
   Oriental Scallop & Pasta Salad, 48
   Santa Fe Salad with Salsa Dressing, 54
   Taco Salad, 65
   Turkey Salad in Phyllo Bowls, 82
   Wheat Berry & Turkey Salad, 51
Salmon,
   Cold Poached Salmon with Lemon-
      Chive Sauce, 71
   Japanese Marinated Salmon Fillets, 70
   Mint-Raspberry Salmon Fillets, 70
Salsa,
   Broiled Tuna Steaks with Kiwi-Papaya
      Salsa, 69
   Corn, Cucumber & Avocado Salsa, 25
   Santa Fe Salad with Salsa Dressing, 54
Sandwiches,
   Barbecued Chicken Sandwich, 96
   California Bean Burgers, 109
   Spicy Pita Sandwich Spread, 109
Santa Fe Salad with Salsa Dressing, 54
Sauces,
   Chunky Italian Meat Sauce, 62
   Corn, Cucumber & Avocado Salsa, 25
   Linguine & Red Clam Sauce, 79
Sausage,
   Turkey Sausage & Bean Soup, 43
Scallops,
   Cumin Citrus Scallops, 79
   Oriental Scallop & Pasta Salad, 48

157

Seafood, 75-79
   Brown Rice & Shrimp Salad, 50
   Cajun Skewered Shrimp, 77
   Chicken & Shrimp Gumbo, 38
   Crab & Cheese-stuffed Phyllo
      Bundles, 29
   Crab Bisque, 40
   Crunchy Crab Salad in Tomato
      Cups, 49
   Cumin Citrus Scallops, 79
   Fats & Cholesterol Comparison, 67
   Jumbo Crab & Cheese-stuffed
      Mushrooms, 78
   Linguine & Red Clam Sauce, 79
   Manhattan Clam Stew, 42
   Oriental Scallop & Pasta Salad, 48
   Shrimp & Basil Pizza, 75
   Shrimp Jambalaya, 77
   Spiced Shrimp Spring Rolls, 28
   Szechuan Shrimp, 76
Seasoned Whole Wheat Tortilla
   Chips, 25
Seasonings,
   Indian Seasoning Medley, 123
   Italian Herb Shaker, 123
   Southwest Seasoning, 123
Sesame Pasta & Vegetables, 125
Sesame Pork, 61
Shrimp,
   Brown Rice & Shrimp Salad, 50
   Cajun Skewered Shrimp, 77
   Chicken & Shrimp Gumbo, 38
   Shrimp & Basil Pizza, 75
   Shrimp Jambalaya, 77
   Spiced Shrimp Spring Rolls, 28
   Szechuan Shrimp, 76
Side Dishes, 120-139
Snacks,
   see: Appetizers & Snacks
Snapper,
   Red Snapper with Mustard Cream
      Sauce, 72
Sole,
   Lemon Dill Sole in Parchment, 72
Soufflés,
   Spinach Soufflé, 118
Soups, 32-43
   Broth Defrosting Chart, 37
   Chicken & Shrimp Gumbo, 38
   Cold Lemon Cucumber Soup, 40
   Creamy Potato & Wild Rice Soup, 39
   Curry Chicken & Apple Soup, 39
   Eggplant Stew, 110
   Frosted Cranberry Soup, 43
   Lentil Stew, 104
   Low-fat Chicken Broth, 36
   Low-fat Vegetable Broth, 35
   Manhattan Clam Stew, 42
   Saffron Squash & Leek Soup, 41
   Turkey Sausage & Bean Soup, 43
   Two Methods to Defat Broth, 37
   Yellow Split Pea & Vegetable Soup, 41
Southern-style Succotash, 136
Southwest Seasoning, 123
Southwestern-style Cauliflower, 132
Spaghetti Squash Primavera, 119
Spiced Chayote & Carrots, 125
Spiced Shrimp Spring Rolls, 28

Spicy Bean & Rice Burrito Bake, 107
Spicy Pita Sandwich Spread, 109
Spinach,
   Cardamom Orange Spinach Salad, 47
   Feta & Spinach-stuffed Chicken
      Breasts, 93
   Lamb & Spinach Pie, 64
   Spinach Soufflé, 118
Spreads,
   Hot Pepper Cheese Spread, 20
   Layered Lentil Loaf, 22
   Spicy Pita Sandwich Spread, 109
   Tropical Fruit & Cheese Log, 24
Spring Rolls,
   Spiced Shrimp Spring Rolls, 28
Squash,
   Orange-gingered Acorn Squash, 124
   Saffron Squash & Leek Soup, 41
   Spaghetti Squash Primavera, 119
Steaks,
   Broiled Tuna Steaks with Kiwi-Papaya
      Salsa, 69
   Italian Herbed Steak Strips, 62
   Pepper Steak Kabobs, 61
   Zesty Mexican Rolled Steak, 64
Stews,
   Eggplant Stew, 110
   Lentil Stew, 104
   Manhattan Clam Stew, 42
Strawberry Tofu Pie, 147
Strawberry-Raspberry Fondue, 145
Stroganoff,
   Mushroom Stroganoff, 117
Succotash,
   Southern-style Succotash, 136
Sweet & Sour Beets, 132
Sweet & Sour Vegetables, 112
Sweet Apple & Poppy Seed
   Dressing, 45
Sweet-spiced Brussels Sprouts
   & Apples, 128
Swordfish,
   Tropical Sweet & Sour Swordfish, 68
Szechuan Shrimp, 76

T

Taco Salad, 65
Tamale Pie, 108
Tandoori Turkey & Rice, 89
Tangerine Yogurt Ice, 146
Tangy Vegetable Dip, 21
Tartar Sauce,
   Fresh Catch with Yogurt Tartar
      Sauce, 74
Tarts,
   Pear Phyllo Tart, 151
Tenderloins,
   Apricot-sauced Turkey Tenderloins, 86
   Pineapple-stuffed Pork Tenderloin, 60
Teriyaki Turkey with Pineapple Rice, 91
Thai-style Skewered Chicken, 27
Thyme,
   Lemon Thyme Chicken with
      Vegetables, 98
Tofu,
   How to Make Ground Tofu, 103

Strawberry Tofu Pie, 147
   Tofu Chili, 114
   Tofu Lo Mein, 116
   Versatile Tofu, 103
Tomatoes,
   Crunchy Crab Salad in Tomato
      Cups, 49
   Mushroom, Celery & Tomato Sauté, 131
   Wild Rice Stuffed Tomatoes, 129
Tortilla Chips,
   Seasoned Whole Wheat Tortilla
      Chips, 25
Tri-bean Bake, 138
Tropical Fruit & Cheese Log, 24
Tropical Papaya Yogurt Ice, 146
Tropical Sweet & Sour Swordfish, 68
Tuna,
   Broiled Tuna Steaks with Kiwi-Papaya
      Salsa, 69
Turkey,
   Apricot-sauced Turkey Tenderloins, 86
   Cider-sauced Turkey Breast, 90
   Herb Turkey Patties with Apple
      Chutney, 89
   Tandoori Turkey & Rice, 89
   Teriyaki Turkey with Pineapple Rice, 91
   Turkey Eggplant Bake, 88
   Turkey Marsala, 87
   Turkey Salad in Phyllo Bowls, 82
   Turkey Sausage & Bean Soup, 43
   Wheat Berry & Turkey Salad, 51
   Wild Rice-filled Turkey Roll, 86
Two Methods to Defat Broth, 37

V

Veal,
   Fats & Cholesterol Comparison, 59
   Veal Scallops with Mandarin Orange
      Sauce, 63
Vegetables,
   also see: names of individual
      vegetables
   Cheese & Vegetable Nachos, 26
   Creamy Chicken & Vegetable
      Casserole, 95
   Creamy Pesto Vegetable Toss, 119
   Garbanzo Bean & Vegetable Pie, 106
   Lemon Thyme Chicken with
      Vegetables, 98
   Low-fat Vegetable Broth, 35
   Molded Vegetable & Saffron Pasta, 138
   Rice & Vegetable Croquettes, 136
   Sesame Pasta & Vegetables, 125
   Sweet & Sour Vegetables, 112
   Tangy Vegetable Dip, 21
   Yellow Split Pea & Vegetable Soup, 41
Vegetarian Main Dishes, 101-119
   Black Bean Chili, 104
   California Bean Burgers, 109
   Creamy Pesto Vegetable Toss, 119
   Eggplant Stew, 110
   Fettucini Alfredo, 113
   Four-cheese Stuffed Manicotti, 113
   How to Match up Complimentary
      Proteins, 101
   Garbanzo Bean & Vegetable Pie, 106

Lasagna Primavera, 115
Lentil Stew, 104
Mexican Pizza with Cornmeal
   Crust, 111
Mexican Seasoned Pinto Beans, 110
Mushroom Stroganoff, 117
Spaghetti Squash Primavera, 119
Spicy Bean & Rice Burrito Bake, 107
Spicy Pita Sandwich Spread, 109
Spinach Soufflé, 118
Sweet & Sour Vegetables, 112
Tamale Pie, 109
Tofu, 103
Tofu Chili, 114
Tofu Lo Mein, 116
Vinegar,
   Low-fat Oil & Vinegar Dressing, 45

W

Wax Beans,
   Green & Wax Beans with Red Pepper
      Purée, 126
Wheat Berry & Turkey Salad, 51
Whole Wheat,
   Seasoned Whole Wheat Tortilla
      Chips, 25
Wild Rice,
   Creamy Potato & Wild Rice Soup, 39
   Wild Rice Stuffed Tomatoes, 129
   Wild Rice-filled Turkey Roll, 86

Y

Yellow Split Pea & Vegetable Soup, 41
Yogurt,
   Fresh Catch with Yogurt Tartar
      Sauce, 74
   Grapefruit Yogurt Ice, 146
   Tangerine Yogurt Ice, 146

Z

Zesty Mexican Rolled Steak, 64